# Maths Practice Year 6

## Question Book

Trevor Dixon

Name _____

Schofield & Sims

# Introduction

The **Schofield & Sims Maths Practice Year 6 Question Book** uses step-by-step practice to develop children's understanding of key mathematical concepts. It covers every Year 6 objective in the 2014 National Curriculum programme of study.

## The structure

This book is split into units, which are based on the key areas of the maths curriculum for Year 6. These are:

- Number and place value
- Fractions, decimals and percentages
- Algebra
- Geometry
- Calculation
- Ratio and proportion
- Measurement
- Statistics.

Each double-page spread follows a consistent 'Practise', 'Extend' and 'Apply' sequence designed to deepen and reinforce learning. Each objective also includes a 'Remember' box that reminds children of the key information needed to help answer the questions.

At the back of the book, there is a 'Final practice' section. Here, mixed questions are used to check children's understanding of the knowledge and skills acquired throughout the book and identify any areas that need to be revisited.

## A mastery approach

The **Primary Practice Maths** series follows a knowledge-based mastery approach. Children deepen their learning by applying and representing their knowledge and skills in multiple ways. This approach reinforces number concepts, nurtures fluency and strengthens both reasoning and problem-solving skills. Integral to this approach is the use of visual representations of mathematical concepts. Some of the most common visual representations used in this book are:

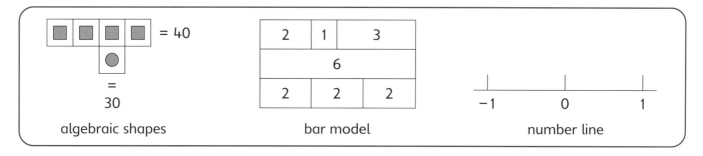

algebraic shapes          bar model          number line

## Assessment and checking progress

A 'Final practice' section is provided at the end of this book to check progress against the Year 6 maths objectives. Children are given a target time of 1 hour to complete this section, which is marked out of 60. Once complete, it enables them to assess their new knowledge and skills independently and to see the areas where they might need more practice.

## Online answers

Answers for every question in the book are available to download from the **Schofield & Sims** website. The answers are accompanied by detailed explanations where helpful. There is also a progress chart, allowing children to track their learning as they complete each set of questions, and an editable certificate.

# Contents

# Number and place value

 **Practise**

**(1)** Write the value of these digits in the number 8 317 596.

    **a.** 3 _____     **b.** 7 _____     **c.** 8 _____

**(2)** Circle the numbers where the digit 4 has a value of four hundred thousand.

    2 498 132     9 240 067     540 400     4 004 004     400     498 065     46 400

**(3)** Circle the numbers where the digit 7 has a value of seven thousand.

    7 000 700     8 764 231     6 357 056     47 920     3 874 790     700     867 034

**(4)** Write the numbers in order from smallest to largest.

    **a.** 2 978 435     2 953 864     2 897 066     2 953 678     2 978 351

    _____

    **b.** 7 034 829     6 924 714     7 040 956     6 923 875     7 034 902

    _____

    **c.** 1 210 865     967 044     970 689     1 119 742     1 208 656

    _____

**(5)** Write the numbers as digits.

    **a.** six million, thirty-two thousand, four hundred and nine     _____

    **b.** five million, four thousand, six hundred and fifty-three     _____

    **c.** one million, one hundred and five thousand and seventy-four     _____

    **d.** two million, nine hundred and seventeen thousand, three hundred     _____

# Extend

**6** Write the correct symbol (< or >) in the circle to compare the numbers.

**a.** 6 023 968 ◯ nine hundred and sixty-five thousand, seven hundred and twenty-seven

**b.** six million, two hundred and five thousand, one hundred and two ◯ 6 206 783

**c.** 3 940 765 ◯ three million, nine hundred and thirty-nine thousand and ninety-one

**7** Write **one** missing digit that would make each number statement correct.

**a.** 4 597 248 < 459 __ 019

**b.** 3 924 070 > 39 __ 6 523

**c.** 79 __ 3610 = 79 836 __ 0

**d.** 252 __ 745 < 2 521 078

> **Tip** There may be more than one possible answer for the questions in **Question 7**.

**8** Use the instructions to write the new number.

**a.** The original number is 4 930 472.

Subtract two hundred thousand and add three hundred. _____

**b.** The original number is 9 271 028.

Add three hundred thousand and subtract one hundred. _____

# Apply

**9** Solve these problems.

**a.** These are the prices of five office blocks. Circle the most expensive office block.

£2 875 000    £2 795 000    £2 799 999    £2 825 000    £2 800 999

**b.** In 2010, the population of a city was 2 572 000. In 2015, the population had increased by three hundred thousand. What was the population in 2015? _____

**c.** Ann will complete a level on her computer game when she has reached one million points. Gold stars are worth 100 000 points and silver stars are worth 10 000 points.

**i.** How many gold stars will Ann need to complete a level? _____

**ii.** How many silver stars will Ann need to complete a level? _____

# Rounding numbers

## Remember

Numbers can be rounded in different ways. When asked to round a number to a specific value, identify the multiples of that value on either side of the number. For example: if rounding 123456 to the nearest 10000, identify 120000 and 130000. Then decide which it is nearer. In this case, 123456 is nearer 120000.

## Practise

(1) Complete the table by rounding the numbers to the values shown.

| Round to the nearest: | 1000 | 10000 | 100000 | 1000000 |
|---|---|---|---|---|
| **a.** 3827458 | | | | |
| **b.** 6173946 | | | | |
| **c.** 4550914 | | | | |
| **d.** 629452 | | | | |
| **e.** 361089 | | | | |

(2) **a.** Write the numbers identified by the letters on these number lines.

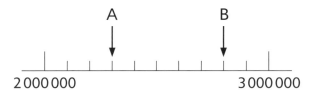
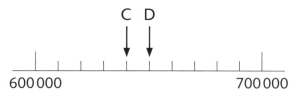

   **i.** A = _____

   **ii.** B = _____

   **iii.** C = _____

   **iv.** D = _____

**b.** Round each answer in **Question 2a** as shown.

   **i.** Round A to the nearest 1000000. _____

   **ii.** Round B to the nearest 1000000. _____

   **iii.** Round C to the nearest 100000. _____

   **iv.** Round D to the nearest 100000. _____

## » Extend

**3** Ben has seven number cards.

| 7 | 1 | 2 | 8 | 4 | 9 | 5 |

**a.** **i.** Write the largest even seven-digit number Ben can make. _____

**ii.** Round this number to the nearest 1000. _____

**iii.** Round this number to the nearest 100 000. _____

**iv.** Round this number to the nearest 1 000 000. _____

**b.** **i.** Write the smallest odd seven-digit number Ben can make. _____

**ii.** Round this number to the nearest 1000. _____

**iii.** Round this number to the nearest 100 000. _____

**iv.** Round this number to the nearest 1 000 000. _____

**4** A number rounded to the nearest 100 000 is 4 200 000.

**a.** What is the largest number it could be? _____

**b.** What is the smallest number it could be? _____

## Apply

**5** Solve these problems.

**a.** The population of a city is 5 175 823. Round the population to the nearest hundred thousand. _____

**b.** A machine in a factory makes 2 756 925 nails a month. How many nails is this to the nearest million? _____

**c.** The distance from the earth to the moon is 384 427 km.

**i.** What is this distance to the nearest ten thousand? _____

**ii.** What is this distance to the nearest hundred thousand? _____

**d.** Light travels at 17 987 547 km/min.

**i.** What is this speed rounded to the nearest hundred thousand km/min? _____

**ii.** What is this speed rounded to the nearest million km/min? _____

# Negative numbers

## Remember

Negative numbers are numbers that are less than 0. Numbers greater than 0 are called positive numbers.

 **Practise**

**1** Find the difference between the two numbers at the ends of the number lines by adding through 0.

**a.**

−6    0    5    _____

**b.**

−8    0    2    _____

**c.**

−7    0    12    _____

**d.**

−11    0    6    _____

**e.**

−8    0    12    _____

**f.**

−12    0    20    _____

**g.**

−8    0    24    _____

**h.**

−25    0    7    _____

**Tip** Count from the negative number to 0 and from 0 to the positive number. Add the two numbers to find the difference.

**2** These buttons in a lift show the floors in a building. Some floors are below ground level. Write how many floors you would move if you travelled between each of the following floors.

**a.** Floor −1 to Floor 5    _____

**b.** Floor −3 to Floor 2    _____

**c.** Floor −4 to Ground Floor    _____

**d.** Floor 7 to Floor −2    _____

**e.** Floor 8 to Floor −3    _____

**f.** Floor −3 to Floor 7    _____

**g.** Floor 6 to Floor −3    _____

8         8
     7
6
     5
4
     3
2
     1
Ground
     −1
−2
     −3
−4

## Extend

**3** Find the difference between these numbers.

    **a.** −5 and 9 _____

    **b.** −10 and 8 _____

    **c.** 14 and −8 _____

    **d.** −14 and 15 _____

**4** Conor records the maximum temperatures inside his greenhouse and the minimum temperatures outside his greenhouse each day for one week.

|  | Sun | Mon | Tue | Wed | Thu | Fri | Sat |
|---|---|---|---|---|---|---|---|
| **Max inside (°C)** | 8 | 7 | 9 | 10 | 7 | 7 | 8 |
| **Min outside (°C)** | −3 | −1 | −4 | −4 | −5 | 0 | −1 |

What was the difference between the maximum temperature inside and the minimum temperature outside the greenhouse on each of these days?

    **a.** Friday _____

    **b.** Tuesday _____

    **c.** Monday _____

    **d.** Saturday _____

## Apply

**5** Choose from the numbers on these six number cards to make these calculations correct.

| 25 | 21 | 16 | 11 | 9 | 8 |
|---|---|---|---|---|---|

    **a.** _____ − _____ = −7

    **b.** _____ − _____ = −14

    **c.** _____ − _____ = −8

    **d.** _____ − _____ = −13

    **e.** _____ − _____ = −9

    **f.** _____ − _____ = −12

**6** Solve these problems.

    **a.** The temperature was 6°C at midday and fell by 10°C by 6 p.m. At midnight, the temperature was −8°C. How much did the temperature fall between 6 p.m. and midnight? _____

    **b.** William has £57 in his bank account. He takes £100 from his account. How much does he owe the bank? _____

    **c.** The lowest point in California is Badwater Basin at −86m below sea level and the highest point is Mount Whitney at 4418m above sea level. What is the difference between the two points? _____

# Estimation

## Remember

Estimating answers is a good way to check if calculations are correct. This is because they give an answer that will be close to the actual answer. Rounding numbers is the best way to estimate an answer before doing a calculation. Doing an inverse operation is a useful way to check an answer after the calculation is complete.

 ## Practise

**(1)** Estimate the answer to the calculation 416 823 + 291 738 by rounding each number:

    **a.** to the nearest hundred thousand. _____ + _____ = _____

    **b.** to the nearest ten thousand. _____ + _____ = _____

    **c.** to the nearest thousand. _____ + _____ = _____

    **d.** to the nearest hundred. _____ + _____ = _____

**(2)** Estimate the answer to the calculation 762 905 − 327 481 by rounding each number:

    **a.** to the nearest hundred thousand. _____ − _____ = _____

    **b.** to the nearest ten thousand. _____ − _____ = _____

    **c.** to the nearest thousand. _____ − _____ = _____

    **d.** to the nearest hundred. _____ − _____ = _____

**(3)** Use an inverse operation to show that these calculations are **not** correct.

    **a.** 42 836 + 36 543 = 78 379 _____

    **b.** 65 094 − 14 384 = 51 710 _____

    **c.** 843 817 + 109 758 = 942 565 _____

    **d.** 510 943 − 304 823 = 216 120 _____

    **e.** 847 834 − 53 421 = 313 624 _____

**Tip** An inverse operation will begin with the answer given in the calculation.

# Extend

**4** Round each large number to the nearest thousand to work out an estimated answer.

    **a.**  69 650 × 7 = _____ × _____ = _____

    **b.**  62 703 ÷ 9 = _____ ÷ _____ = _____

    **c.**  108 278 ÷ 12 = _____ ÷ _____ = _____

**5** Write how much the estimated answers differ from the actual answers.

    **a.**  The numbers in the calculation 26 204 + 18 308 are
        rounded to 26 000 + 18 000.                  _____

    **b.**  The numbers in the calculation 49 365 − 22 577 are
        rounded to 50 000 − 23 000.                  _____

# Apply

**6** Round the numbers in these calculations to work out an estimated answer.

    **a.**  805 722 − 38 543 = _____ − _____ = _____

    **b.**  4890 × 67 = _____ × _____ = _____

    **c.**  4876 ÷ 49 = _____ ÷ _____ = _____

> **Tip** Always round to a number that can be used for a mental calculation.

**7** Solve these problems.

    **a.**  Theo measures the capacity of a glass. It holds 410ml. Theo has a three-litre bottle
        of juice. Use an estimated calculation to find how many glasses he can fill.

        _____ ÷ _____ = _____

    **b.**  Erin buys 15 party invitation cards. Each card costs 39p. Use an estimated calculation
        to find how many pounds this will cost.

        _____ × _____ = _____

    **c.**  Ethan has a two-kilogram box of dog food. Each day he feeds his dog 240g of the
        food. Use an estimated calculation to find how many portions he can feed his dog.

        _____ ÷ _____ = _____

# Special numbers

## Remember

There are some numbers that are special numbers. A common multiple is a number that is a multiple of two or more numbers. A common factor is a number that is a factor of two or more numbers. A prime number is a number with exactly two factors (1 and itself).

 **Practise**

**(1)** For each number, list the multiples that are less than 100. Circle the common multiples for each pair.

    **a.**  6 and 9

        Multiples of 6: _____

        Multiples of 9: _____

    **b.**  12 and 15

        Multiples of 12: _____

        Multiples of 15: _____

**(2)** List the factors of these pairs of numbers. Circle the common factors.

    **a.**  48 and 60

        Factors of 48: _____

        Factors of 60: _____

    **b.**  42 and 56

        Factors of 42: _____

        Factors of 56: _____

**(3)** Complete prime factor trees to show the prime factors of the numbers in the circle.

    **a.**

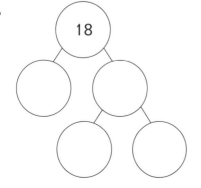

    **b.**

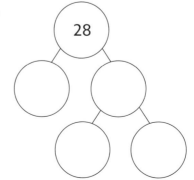

# Extend

**4** Find the lowest common multiple of these pairs of numbers.

    **a.** 4 and 10 _____        **b.** 3 and 6 _____

**Tip** The lowest common multiple is the smallest number of a set of common multiples.

**5** Find all the common factors of these pairs of numbers.

    **a.** 24 and 36 _____

    **b.** 36 and 54 _____

**6** Find the highest common factor of these pairs of numbers.

    **a.** 36 and 54 _____        **b.** 48 and 60 _____

**Tip** The highest common factor is the largest number of a set of common factors.

# Apply

**7** Find **three** pairs of prime numbers that add together to give 30.

    **a.** _____ + _____    **b.** _____ + _____    **c.** _____ + _____

**8** Solve these problems.

    **a.** Harrison is sticking cards into two albums. He puts 72 cards into one and 90 cards into the other. Every page has the same number of cards. What is the greatest number of cards that he could put on a page? _____

    **b.** At a railway station, trains travelling north arrive every 15 minutes and trains travelling south arrive every 25 minutes. If two trains arrive at 14:45, what is the next time that two trains arrive at the station together? _____

    **c.** A farmer has fewer than 100 eggs and must sort them into boxes of 6, 8 or 15. When he puts them in boxes of 6 or 8, there are 3 eggs left over. When he puts them into boxes of 15, there are none left over. How many eggs does the farmer have? _____

# Multiplication and division

## Remember

Using column multiplication is an efficient method for multiplying larger numbers. Using a division box is an efficient method for dividing larger numbers. Long division records the method to find the remainders within the division. Short division uses mental arithmetic to find the answer.

**Set out the multiplication in place value columns:**

```
      3   6   7
×         2   3
─────────────────
  1   1₂  0₂  1
  7₁  3₁  4   0
─────────────────
  8   4   4   1
```

**Set out the division in a division box:**

```
              2   3
         ─────────────
    24 │  5   5   2        Divide from the left.
       −  4   8            55 tens ÷ 24 =
         ─────────           2 tens r.7 tens
              7   2        Exchange 7 tens for 70 ones.
       −      7   2        72 ones ÷ 24 =
         ─────────
                  0         3 ones r.0
```

## Practise

(1) Complete these calculations using column multiplication.

    **a.** $74 \times 24 =$ _____

    **b.** $49 \times 34 =$ _____

    **c.** $250 \times 28 =$ _____

    **d.** $245 \times 29 =$ _____

    **e.** $314 \times 42 =$ _____

    **f.** $522 \times 36 =$ _____

(2) Complete these calculations using long division.

    **a.** $1744 \div 4 =$ _____

    **b.** $759 \div 23 =$ _____

    **c.** $432 \div 18 =$ _____

    **d.** $945 \div 21 =$ _____

    **e.** $792 \div 22 =$ _____

    **f.** $416 \div 16 =$ _____

(3) Complete these calculations using short division.

    **a.** $780 \div 20 =$ _____

    **b.** $625 \div 25 =$ _____

    **c.** $640 \div 40 =$ _____

    **d.** $575 \div 25 =$ _____

    **e.** $590 \div 20 =$ _____

    **f.** $960 \div 60 =$ _____

# Extend

**4** Find the missing number in each pair of calculations.

    **a.** $45 \times 36 =$ _____ $\times 30$         **b.** $1536 \div 24 = 1600 \div$ _____

    **c.** $128 \times 26 =$ _____ $\times 32$       **d.** $2184 \div 52 = 4410 \div$ _____

**5** Use the first calculation to solve the second calculation.

    **a.** $365 \times 24 = 8760$    so   $365 \times 48 =$ _____

    **b.** $824 \times 35 = 28840$   so   $412 \times 35 =$ _____

    **c.** $6400 \div 32 = 200$    so   $6400 \div 16 =$ _____

    **d.** $8250 \div 66 = 125$    so   $16500 \div 66 =$ _____

# Apply

**6** These calculations are **not** correct. Explain the error.

    **a.**
```
          4   3   6
      ×       6   3
    ─────────────────
      1   3₁  0₁  8
      2   6₂  1₃  6
    ─────────────────
      3   9   2   4
              1
```

    **b.**
```
              8   2   4
          ×       6   5
        ─────────────────
          4   1₁  2₂  0
      4   9₁  4₂  4   0
        ─────────────────
      4   3   5   6   0
          1
```

    _____       _____

    _____       _____

**7** A number is divided by 45 and the answer is 132r.26. What was the number?

    _____

**8** A three-digit number is multiplied by a two-digit number. All the digits are the same. The answer is 30525. What is the calculation?

    _____ $\times$ _____

# Number word problems

Extend

## Remember

Read the word problem carefully to understand what it is asking for. Decide the order needed to complete the calculation if it is more than a one-step problem. Make sure to use the correct numbers and operations to solve the problem. Remember to check the calculation.

## Practise

**1** Solve these problems.

**a.** A rugby ground can hold 27 486 people. On match day, there are 19 538 people in the ground. How many more people could fit into the ground? _____

**b.** On a cruise ship, there are 1348 cabins for two passengers and 374 cabins for four passengers. There is also a crew of 1284.

    **i.** How many passengers are there? _____

    **ii.** How many people are on board the cruise ship? _____

**c.** There are 504 seats on a train. The train has six identical carriages.

    **i.** How many seats are in each carriage? _____

    **ii.** There are 387 passengers with seats on the train. How many empty seats are there? _____

**d.** A supermarket gets a delivery of 1560 tins of soup on Mondays, Wednesdays, Thursdays and Saturdays. How many tins of soup are delivered each week? _____

**e.** Anna is organising a trip for 807 football supporters. She books some coaches with 55 seats.

    **i.** How many coaches will she need to book? _____

    **ii.** How many spare seats will there be? _____

**f.** Jacob is buying some packs of paper for a school. He can buy 50 packs of 500 sheets for the same price as 30 packs of 750 sheets. How many more sheets will he get if he buys 50 packs of 500 sheets? _____

# ⟫ Extend

**2** Solve these problems.

**a.** Over the last year, Raj has bought 84 packs of superhero cards at £2.99 each. Each pack contains 12 cards.

    **i.** How much has Raj spent on the cards? _____

Raj gives away spare cards to his friends. He has 672 cards left.

    **ii.** How many cards did he give away? _____

He puts the cards he has left into an album. There are 8 cards on a page.

    **iii.** How many pages did Raj fill? _____

**b.** A factory has five machines making pencils. The three small machines can each make 3270 pencils an hour and the two large machines can each make 5175 pencils an hour. The factory works for 12 hours a day.

    **i.** How many pencils are made in one working day? _____

    **ii.** If the pencils are put into packs of 6, how many packs are filled in a day? _____

# Apply

**3** Aisha investigates calculating with different numbers. Tick to show whether Aisha's statements are always, sometimes or never true.

| | | Always true | Sometimes true | Never true |
|---|---|---|---|---|
| **a.** | Adding a four-digit even number and a three-digit odd number gives an odd answer. | | | |
| **b.** | Subtracting a three-digit number from a four-digit number gives a two- or three-digit answer. | | | |
| **c.** | Multiplying a four-digit number by an odd number gives an odd answer. | | | |
| **d.** | Dividing a four-digit number by a two-digit number can give a one-digit answer. | | | |

**4** A factory is making candles for gift shops. There are 24 candles in a box. The factory fills 286 full boxes and there are 17 candles left over.

**a.** How many candles were made? _____

**b.** The factory makes another 1087 candles. Along with the leftover candles, how many more boxes can they fill? _____

# Order of operations

## Remember

When a calculation uses more than one operation, there is an order to complete the individual operations. Remember this order by using the acronym BIDMAS.

| B | I | D | M | A | S |
|---|---|---|---|---|---|
| Brackets | Indices | Division and Multiplication | | Addition and Subtraction | |

For example:

| Calculation | Using BIDMAS | |
|---|---|---|
| $10^2 + (10 - 6) \times 6 \div 2 =$ | Complete the calculation in the brackets. | $(10 - 6) = 4$ |
| $10^2 + 4 \times 6 \div 2 =$ | Complete any calculation with indices. | $10^2 = 10 \times 10 = 100$ |
| $100 + 4 \times 6 \div 2 =$ | Complete any division and multiplication calculations in the order they appear. | $4 \times 6 \div 2 = 24 \div 2 = 12$ |
| $100 + 12 = 112$ | Complete any addition and subtraction calculations in the order they appear. | |

## Practise

**(1)** Calculate:

**a.** $8 + 20 \div 4 =$ _____

**b.** $30 - 6 \div 3 =$ _____

**c.** $15 + 15 \times 2 =$ _____

**d.** $40 - 10 \times 2 =$ _____

**e.** $30 \div 5 + 5 =$ _____

**f.** $36 \div 3 + 9 =$ _____

**g.** $8 \times 6 + 3 =$ _____

**h.** $10 \times 8 - 4 =$ _____

**i.** $24 \div 4 \times 2 =$ _____

**j.** $24 \times 4 \div 2 =$ _____

**k.** $5 + 15 \div 5 =$ _____

**l.** $24 - 12 \div 3 =$ _____

**(2)** Complete these calculations with brackets.

**a.** $(8 + 20) \div 4 =$ _____

**b.** $(30 - 6) \div 3 =$ _____

**c.** $(15 + 15) \times 2 =$ _____

**d.** $(40 - 10) \times 2 =$ _____

**e.** $30 \div (5 + 5) =$ _____

**f.** $36 \div (3 + 9) =$ _____

**g.** $8 \times (6 + 3) =$ _____

**h.** $10 \times (8 - 4) =$ _____

**i.** $24 \div (4 \times 2) =$ _____

**j.** $24 \times (4 \div 2) =$ _____

**k.** $10 \times (5 - 2) =$ _____

**l.** $(10 - 5) \times 2 =$ _____

## Extend

**3** Complete these calculations with indices.

    **a.** $6 + 5 \times 4 - 3^2 =$ _____

    **b.** $8 - 12 \div 6 + 5^2 =$ _____

    **c.** $12 \times 2^3 - 48 \div 2^2 =$ _____

    **d.** $10 + 20 \times 20 + 10^2 =$ _____

    **e.** $5^2 \times 2^2 - 10^2 =$ _____

    **f.** $40 - 20 \div 2^2 + 20 =$ _____

**4** Calculate:

    **a.** $(6 + 5) \times 4 - 3^2 =$ _____

    **b.** $(48 - 12) \div (3^2) =$ _____

    **c.** $(4^3 + 2^3) \div (3^2 + 3^3) =$ _____

    **d.** $(10 + 20) \times 20 + 10^2 =$ _____

    **e.** $(5^2 + 15) \div (24 - 2^2) =$ _____

    **f.** $(40 - 20) \div 2^2 + 20 =$ _____

 ## Apply

**5** Circle the calculation in each set that is correct.

    **a.** $24 + 6 \div 3 - 2 = 8$      $(24 + 6) \div 3 - 2 = 8$      $24 + 6 \div (3 - 2) = 8$

    **b.** $(40 - 5) \times (2 + 2) = 20$      $(40 - 5) \times 2 + 2 = 20$      $40 - 5 \times (2 + 2) = 20$

> **Tip**   Calculate each equation to find the correct answer. Remember BIDMAS rules.

**6** Add **one** pair of brackets to these equations to make them correct.

    **a.** $20 + 5 \times 4 + 6 = 70$      **b.** $80 - 20 \div 2 - 1 = 29$

    **c.** $25 \times 5 + 5 - 5 = 245$      **d.** $30 + 6 \div 2 \times 3 = 31$

    **e.** $16 + 24 \div 4 \times 2 = 19$      **f.** $10 \times 10 \div 10 + 10 = 110$

**7** Maryam uses two baking trays to bake a set of cupcakes. One tray holds 8 cupcakes and the other holds 6. She bakes 3 sets of cupcakes. How many cupcakes will she bake? Circle all the expressions that will solve the problem.

     $3 \times 8 + 6$      $3 (8 + 6)$      $3 \times 8 + 3 \times 6$      $8 + 6 \times 3$      $(6 + 8) \times 3$

# Equivalent fractions

Extend

## Remember

Equivalent fractions are fractions that have different numerators and denominators but have the same value.

Sometimes it is possible to rewrite a fraction using numbers with smaller values as the numerator and denominator. This is called simplifying the fraction or reducing it to its lowest terms.

For example: $\frac{12}{20} = \frac{3}{5}$   Find a common factor of the numerator (12) and the denominator (20). The common factor needed here is 4. Divide the numerator by 4 (12 ÷ 4 = 3) and the denominator by 4 (20 ÷ 4 = 5).

It is also possible to write a fraction using numerators and denominators of a larger value.

For example: $\frac{5}{8} = \frac{15}{24}$   Use the same number to multiply the numerator and denominator. Here they have both been multiplied by 3.

## ✏️ Practise

**1** Simplify these fractions using a common factor.

a. $\frac{10}{12} = \frac{5}{6}$

b. $\frac{8}{12} = \frac{4}{6}$

c. $\frac{8}{16} =$ _____

d. $\frac{15}{20} = \frac{7.5}{10}$

e. $\frac{6}{18} = \frac{3}{9}$

f. $\frac{18}{20} = \frac{9}{10}$

g. $\frac{4}{18} = \frac{2}{9}$

h. $\frac{10}{25} =$ _____

i. $\frac{40}{100} = \frac{20}{50}$

**2** Change these fractions to make them equivalent. The denominator of the fraction is shown.

a. $\frac{3}{4} = \frac{}{24}$

b. $\frac{2}{3} = \frac{}{12}$

c. $\frac{3}{5} = \frac{}{15}$

d. $\frac{3}{10} = \frac{}{20}$

e. $\frac{4}{5} = \frac{}{30}$

f. $\frac{7}{25} = \frac{}{100}$

**3** Change these fractions to make them equivalent. The numerator of the fraction is shown.

a. $\frac{3}{4} = \frac{15}{}$

b. $\frac{2}{5} = \frac{10}{}$

c. $\frac{1}{6} = \frac{5}{}$

d. $\frac{5}{12} = \frac{10}{}$

e. $\frac{5}{6} = \frac{25}{}$

f. $\frac{7}{20} = \frac{35}{}$

**Extend**

(4) Find the missing numerators and denominators in these equivalent fractions.

a. $\dfrac{\phantom{6}}{8} = \dfrac{6}{16} = \dfrac{12}{\phantom{16}}$

b. $\dfrac{\phantom{4}}{5} = \dfrac{4}{10} = \dfrac{16}{\phantom{16}}$

c. $\dfrac{2}{3} = \dfrac{8}{\phantom{8}} = \dfrac{\phantom{8}}{36}$

d. $\dfrac{10}{25} = \dfrac{\phantom{5}}{5} = \dfrac{40}{\phantom{40}}$

(5) Write these fractions in the table to show how they can simplify.

| | | | | | | | | | |
|---|---|---|---|---|---|---|---|---|---|
| $\dfrac{21}{35}$ | $\dfrac{25}{40}$ | $\dfrac{21}{28}$ | $\dfrac{30}{48}$ | $\dfrac{16}{24}$ | $\dfrac{24}{32}$ | $\dfrac{27}{45}$ | $\dfrac{24}{36}$ | $\dfrac{45}{72}$ | $\dfrac{24}{40}$ |

| Simplify to $\dfrac{2}{3}$ | Simplify to $\dfrac{3}{4}$ | Simplify to $\dfrac{3}{5}$ | Simplify to $\dfrac{5}{8}$ |
|---|---|---|---|
| | | | |

(6) Write the three fractions in each set with the same lowest common denominator.

a. $\dfrac{2}{3}$ $\qquad$ $\dfrac{4}{5}$ $\qquad$ $\dfrac{3}{10}$

b. $\dfrac{7}{8}$ $\qquad$ $\dfrac{5}{6}$ $\qquad$ $\dfrac{1}{12}$

_____

_____

 **Apply**

(7) Solve these problems. Write each answer as a fraction in its simplest terms.

a. Kyra has 50 crayons. 15 of the crayons are red. What fraction of the crayons are red? _____

b. Amil is driving 125km. He has driven 75km. What fraction of the journey has he driven? _____

c. Zack has 240 sheep. 168 of the sheep are white. What fraction of the sheep are white? _____

d. Alex listens to 175 songs. 35 of the songs are by the same person. What fraction is this? _____

(8) Circle the fraction in each set that is **not** equivalent.

a. $\dfrac{12}{15}$ $\qquad$ $\dfrac{28}{35}$ $\qquad$ $\dfrac{27}{33}$ $\qquad$ $\dfrac{24}{30}$

b. $\dfrac{25}{30}$ $\qquad$ $\dfrac{35}{40}$ $\qquad$ $\dfrac{21}{24}$ $\qquad$ $\dfrac{42}{48}$

# Comparing and ordering fractions

## Remember

To compare fractions easily, they must have the same denominator. This means that fractions must be changed so they all have a common denominator. Fractions can then be compared using the numerators of the fractions. For example: to write $\frac{7}{10}$, $\frac{3}{4}$ and $\frac{1}{2}$ in order from smallest to largest, change the fractions so they have a common denominator of 20.

$$\frac{7}{10} = \frac{14}{20} \qquad \frac{3}{4} = \frac{15}{20} \qquad \frac{1}{2} = \frac{10}{20}$$

The fractions in order from smallest to largest are: $\frac{1}{2}$ $\quad$ $\frac{7}{10}$ $\quad$ $\frac{3}{4}$

## Practise

**1** Write the correct symbol (<, > or =) in the circle to compare these fractions.

a. $\frac{1}{2}$ $\bigcirc$ $\frac{3}{5}$    b. $\frac{3}{4}$ $\bigcirc$ $\frac{5}{6}$    c. $\frac{5}{6}$ $\bigcirc$ $\frac{2}{3}$

d. $\frac{12}{18}$ $\bigcirc$ $\frac{16}{24}$    e. $\frac{9}{25}$ $\bigcirc$ $\frac{1}{5}$    f. $\frac{7}{8}$ $\bigcirc$ $\frac{2}{3}$

g. $\frac{5}{12}$ $\bigcirc$ $\frac{1}{3}$    h. $\frac{7}{10}$ $\bigcirc$ $\frac{21}{30}$    i. $\frac{6}{18}$ $\bigcirc$ $\frac{8}{24}$

j. $\frac{25}{30}$ $\bigcirc$ $\frac{15}{18}$    k. $\frac{8}{28}$ $\bigcirc$ $\frac{6}{14}$    l. $\frac{10}{16}$ $\bigcirc$ $\frac{21}{28}$

**2** Write these fractions in order from smallest to largest.

a. $\frac{5}{8}$ $\qquad$ $\frac{7}{12}$ $\qquad$ $\frac{1}{2}$ _____

b. $\frac{7}{10}$ $\qquad$ $\frac{3}{5}$ $\qquad$ $\frac{3}{4}$ _____

c. $\frac{11}{16}$ $\qquad$ $\frac{5}{8}$ $\qquad$ $\frac{3}{4}$ _____

d. $\frac{5}{6}$ $\qquad$ $\frac{7}{9}$ $\qquad$ $\frac{2}{3}$ _____

e. $\frac{2}{3}$ $\qquad$ $\frac{11}{15}$ $\qquad$ $\frac{3}{5}$ _____

**Tip** Change the fractions so that they have a common denominator.

# Extend

**3** Write the correct symbol (<, > or =) in the circle to compare these fractions.

a. $\frac{3}{20}$ ◯ $\frac{2}{5}$ ◯ $\frac{1}{2}$

b. $\frac{2}{3}$ ◯ $\frac{5}{9}$ ◯ $\frac{7}{18}$

c. $\frac{7}{8}$ ◯ $\frac{3}{4}$ ◯ $\frac{7}{12}$

d. $\frac{2}{5}$ ◯ $\frac{19}{30}$ ◯ $\frac{7}{10}$

**4** These fractions are in order. Write the missing numerators.

a. $\frac{7}{10}$ > $\frac{\rule{1cm}{0.4pt}}{20}$ > $\frac{3}{5}$

b. $\frac{1}{2}$ > $\frac{\rule{1cm}{0.4pt}}{9}$ > $\frac{1}{3}$

c. $\frac{5}{8}$ < $\frac{\rule{1cm}{0.4pt}}{16}$ < $\frac{3}{4}$

d. $\frac{3}{4}$ < $\frac{\rule{1cm}{0.4pt}}{24}$ < $\frac{5}{6}$

> **Tip** Find a common denominator for the fractions in the sequence, then work out the missing numerator.

# Apply

**5** Solve these problems.

a. Martin, Nisha and Bess have homework. They do the work on Saturday and Sunday. On Saturday, Martin has done $\frac{5}{12}$ of his homework, Nisha has done $\frac{3}{8}$, and Bess has done $\frac{13}{24}$. Who has the most homework to do on Sunday? _____

b. In a pot of crayons, $\frac{5}{24}$ are red, $\frac{1}{4}$ are blue, $\frac{3}{8}$ are green and $\frac{1}{6}$ are yellow. Which colour crayons are there most of? _____

c. Ned, Arjun and Sasha complete a quiz. Ned got $\frac{7}{10}$ of the questions right, Arjun got $\frac{19}{25}$ right and Sasha got $\frac{37}{50}$ right. Who got the most questions right? _____

d. Three friends share a pizza. Jess says she has eaten $\frac{3}{8}$ of the pizza, Lisa says she has eaten $\frac{7}{24}$ and Ken says he has eaten $\frac{5}{12}$.

Explain why this is **not** possible.

_____

_____

# Adding and subtracting fractions

## Remember

When adding or subtracting fractions, it is important that the fractions have the same denominator so that equivalent fractions can be used.

For example:

$\frac{2}{3} + \frac{4}{5} =$ Change the fractions so they have a common denominator.

$\frac{2}{3} = \frac{10}{15}$ $\frac{4}{5} = \frac{12}{15}$ The common denominator for thirds and fifths is 15.

$\frac{10}{15} + \frac{12}{15} = \frac{22}{15} = 1\frac{7}{15}$

When subtracting fractions, it is good practice to either use a number line or change mixed numbers to improper fractions.

For example:

$2\frac{3}{8} - 1\frac{5}{6} =$ Change the fractions so that they have a common denominator.

$\frac{3}{8} = \frac{9}{24}$ $\frac{5}{6} = \frac{20}{24}$ The common denominator for eighths and sixths is 24.

$2\frac{9}{24} - 1\frac{20}{24} =$ Change to improper fractions.

$\frac{57}{24} - \frac{44}{24} = \frac{13}{24}$

## Practise

**(1)** Complete these additions.

**a.** $\frac{5}{6} + \frac{2}{3} =$ _____   **b.** $\frac{7}{8} + \frac{1}{2} =$ _____   **c.** $\frac{3}{4} + \frac{5}{6} =$ _____

**d.** $\frac{1}{2} + \frac{7}{10} =$ _____   **e.** $\frac{2}{3} + \frac{1}{4} =$ _____   **f.** $\frac{4}{5} + \frac{1}{3} =$ _____

**(2)** Complete these subtractions.

**a.** $\frac{4}{5} - \frac{3}{10} =$ _____   **b.** $\frac{18}{25} - \frac{2}{5} =$ _____   **c.** $\frac{5}{6} - \frac{2}{5} =$ _____

**d.** $\frac{2}{3} - \frac{3}{8} =$ _____   **e.** $\frac{11}{12} - \frac{2}{9} =$ _____   **f.** $\frac{2}{3} - \frac{3}{10} =$ _____

**(3)** Complete these calculations with mixed numbers.

**a.** $2\frac{1}{3} + 3\frac{3}{8} =$ _____   **b.** $2\frac{2}{5} + 1\frac{3}{4} =$ _____   **c.** $3\frac{1}{3} - 1\frac{3}{4} =$ _____

**d.** $4\frac{2}{5} - 3\frac{3}{4} =$ _____   **e.** $2\frac{1}{6} + 3\frac{3}{5} =$ _____   **f.** $2\frac{2}{3} + 1\frac{2}{5} =$ _____

**Extend**

(4) Find the missing fractions.

**a.** $\frac{7}{10} + $ _____ $= 1\frac{1}{4}$

**b.** $2\frac{3}{5} + $ _____ $= 3\frac{1}{4}$

**c.** $\frac{7}{8} - $ _____ $= \frac{2}{3}$

**d.** $4\frac{1}{12} - $ _____ $= 2\frac{1}{2}$

**e.** _____ $+ \frac{3}{4} + \frac{3}{5} = 1\frac{7}{20}$

**f.** _____ $+ \frac{7}{8} + \frac{5}{6} = 2$

(5) Use these number cards to make the two fractions missing from each calculation. Use each card once in each calculation.

**a.** _____ $+$ _____ $= 1\frac{7}{15}$

**b.** _____ $+$ _____ $= 1\frac{3}{20}$

**c.** _____ $-$ _____ $= \frac{7}{20}$

**d.** _____ $-$ _____ $= \frac{2}{15}$

**Tip** The two denominators in the calculation have been used to find a common denominator. Use your knowledge of factors to find the original denominators.

 **Apply**

(6) Solve these problems.

**a.** Henry has three days to complete his homework. On the first day, he completes $\frac{3}{8}$ of his homework and on the second day, he completes another $\frac{2}{5}$. What fraction must he complete on the third day to finish his work?

**b.** Zaid has a bag of sweets. He eats $\frac{1}{10}$ of the sweets. He gives $\frac{1}{8}$ of the sweets each to 3 friends. What fraction of the bag does he have left?

**c.** Penny is planting bulbs in the park. She plants $4\frac{2}{3}$ bags on Monday and $3\frac{3}{10}$ bags on Tuesday. How many bags does she plant altogether?

**d.** Noor is on a walk. The walk is $11\frac{3}{5}$ km altogether. She walks $4\frac{1}{2}$ km, then stops for a rest. She then walks another $5\frac{3}{4}$ km. How much further does she have to walk? _____

# Multiplying and dividing fractions

## Remember

To multiply two fractions, multiply the numerators then multiply the denominators. Some answers will need to be simplified. For example:

$$\frac{3}{5} \times \frac{2}{3} = \frac{3 \times 2}{5 \times 3} = \frac{6}{15} = \frac{2}{5}$$

To divide a fraction by a whole number, multiply the denominator by the whole number. Some answers will need to be simplified. For example:

$$\frac{2}{3} \div 4 = \frac{2}{3 \times 4} = \frac{2}{12} = \frac{1}{6}$$

 ## Practise

**(1)** Multiply these fractions.

**a.** $\frac{1}{3} \times \frac{1}{6} =$ _____

**b.** $\frac{1}{3} \times \frac{3}{8} =$ _____

**c.** $\frac{1}{3} \times \frac{1}{8} =$ _____

**d.** $\frac{2}{3} \times \frac{1}{8} =$ _____

**e.** $\frac{2}{5} \times \frac{1}{4} =$ _____

**f.** $\frac{2}{3} \times \frac{1}{4} =$ _____

**g.** $\frac{3}{5} \times \frac{1}{2} =$ _____

**h.** $\frac{3}{4} \times \frac{1}{5} =$ _____

**i.** $\frac{4}{5} \times \frac{2}{3} =$ _____

**j.** $\frac{7}{8} \times \frac{1}{2} =$ _____

**k.** $\frac{3}{8} \times \frac{3}{4} =$ _____

**l.** $\frac{3}{10} \times \frac{1}{2} =$ _____

**(2)** Divide these fractions.

**a.** $\frac{5}{6} \div 4 =$ _____

**b.** $\frac{3}{8} \div 3 =$ _____

**c.** $\frac{1}{6} \div 3 =$ _____

**d.** $\frac{3}{4} \div 3 =$ _____

**e.** $\frac{2}{5} \div 4 =$ _____

**f.** $\frac{4}{5} \div 2 =$ _____

**g.** $\frac{3}{5} \div 3 =$ _____

**h.** $\frac{3}{8} \div 4 =$ _____

**i.** $\frac{1}{10} \div 10 =$ _____

**j.** $\frac{5}{6} \div 2 =$ _____

**k.** $\frac{1}{4} \div 5 =$ _____

**l.** $\frac{5}{12} \div 2 =$ _____

**Tip** When you have completed the multiplication or the division, check to see if the answer can be simplified.

**Extend**

**3** Find the missing numbers.

**a.** $\dfrac{1}{3} \times \dfrac{1}{\rule{2em}{0.4pt}} = \dfrac{1}{15}$  **b.** $\dfrac{\rule{2em}{0.4pt}}{4} \times \dfrac{3}{4} = \dfrac{3}{16}$  **c.** $\dfrac{2}{\rule{2em}{0.4pt}} \times \dfrac{2}{5} = \dfrac{4}{25}$

**d.** $\dfrac{2}{5} \times \dfrac{3}{\rule{2em}{0.4pt}} = \dfrac{6}{25}$  **e.** $\dfrac{\rule{2em}{0.4pt}}{4} \times \dfrac{3}{\rule{2em}{0.4pt}} = \dfrac{9}{20}$  **f.** $\dfrac{4}{\rule{2em}{0.4pt}} \times \dfrac{\rule{2em}{0.4pt}}{3} = \dfrac{8}{15}$

**4** Find the missing numbers.

**a.** $\dfrac{1}{\rule{2em}{0.4pt}} \div 5 = \dfrac{1}{10}$  **b.** $\dfrac{\rule{2em}{0.4pt}}{4} \div 5 = \dfrac{7}{20}$  **c.** $\dfrac{2}{5} \div \rule{3em}{0.4pt} = \dfrac{2}{15}$

**d.** $\dfrac{3}{\rule{2em}{0.4pt}} \div 3 = \dfrac{3}{21}$  **e.** $\dfrac{2}{\rule{2em}{0.4pt}} \div 5 = \dfrac{2}{35}$  **f.** $\dfrac{\rule{2em}{0.4pt}}{8} \div 2 = \dfrac{3}{16}$

**5** The answers to these calculations have been simplified. What could the missing numbers be?

**a.** $\dfrac{1}{8} \times \dfrac{2}{\rule{2em}{0.4pt}} = \dfrac{1}{12}$  **b.** $\dfrac{4}{\rule{2em}{0.4pt}} \div 8 = \dfrac{1}{10}$  **c.** $\rule{3em}{0.4pt} \div 3 = \dfrac{1}{4}$

**Tip** Use equivalent fractions of the answers to find the missing numbers.

 **Apply**

**6** Solve these problems.

**a.** Farid is cutting out a small rectangular flower bed from a lawn. The flower bed is $\frac{3}{4}$m long and $\frac{4}{5}$m wide. What is the area of the flower bed?  _____

**b.** Ayesha has a bag of flour that is $\frac{4}{5}$ full. She uses the flour to bake 4 similar small cakes. What fraction of the bag is used for each small cake?  _____

**c.** Kelly has 5 bags and puts $\frac{2}{5}$kg of sweets into each of them.

   **i.** How many kilograms does she use to fill the five bags?  _____

   **ii.** Kelly takes one of the bags with $\frac{2}{5}$kg of sweets and divides it between four friends. What fraction of a kilogram of sweets does each friend get?  _____

**d.** In an orchestra, $\frac{3}{5}$ of the children play a stringed instrument. Of these children, $\frac{2}{3}$ play a violin. What fraction of the orchestra play the violin?  _____

# Decimals

## Remember

A decimal number is a number that is based on groups of ten.

| TTh | Th | H | T | O | . | t | h | th |
|-----|-----|-----|-----|-----|-----|-----|-----|-----|
|  |  |  |  | 0 | . | 3 | 7 | 2 |

Here is the number 0.372. $0.372 = \frac{3}{10} + \frac{7}{100} + \frac{2}{1000} = \frac{372}{1000}$

Multiplying a number by 10, 100 or 1000 moves the digits of the number 1, 2 or 3 places to the left. For example: $2.801 \times 1000 = 2801$

Dividing a number by 10, 100 or 1000 moves the digits of the number 1, 2 or 3 places to the right. For example: $403 \div 1000 = 0.403$

## Practise

(1) Write the value of the digit 7 in each number.

    **a.** 325.87 _____

    **b.** 3.087 _____

    **c.** 2971.83 _____

    **d.** 4.837 _____

    **e.** 1954.7 _____

    **f.** 6.537 _____

(2) **a.** Circle the numbers where the digit 8 has a value of eight hundredths.

    68.92      2.085      1967.8      32.98      0.768      4924.681

    **b.** Circle the numbers where the digit 2 has a value of two thousandths.

    3.042      2044      31.427      198.52      56.932      0.862

(3) Calculate:

    **a.** $4.7 \times 100 =$ _____

    **b.** $83.08 \div 10 =$ _____

    **c.** $9765 \div 100 =$ _____

    **d.** $5.936 \times 1000 =$ _____

    **e.** $0.09 \times 1000 =$ _____

    **f.** $28 \div 1000 =$ _____

    **g.** $0.006 \times 100 =$ _____

    **h.** $90.1 \times 100 =$ _____

## Extend

**4** Write each set of fractions as one fraction and one decimal.

**a.** $\frac{9}{10} + \frac{2}{1000} + \frac{7}{100} =$ _____ = _____

**b.** $\frac{1}{1000} + \frac{6}{10} + \frac{9}{100} =$ _____ = _____

**c.** $\frac{3}{100} + \frac{7}{1000} + \frac{2}{10} =$ _____ = _____

**d.** $\frac{9}{1000} + \frac{3}{100} =$ _____ = _____

> **Tip** Make sure the digits for the numerators are written in the correct place value column. It may help to use a place value chart.

**5** Find the missing number.

**a.** $10.08 \times$ _____ $= 1008$

**b.** $345 \div$ _____ $= 0.345$

**c.** _____ $\div 1000 = 7.032$

**d.** _____ $\times 100 = 200.5$

## Apply

**6** Use these four number cards to write a number between:

| 2 | 3 | 6 | 7 |

**a.** 3.5 and 3.75 _____

**b.** 6.29 and 6.801 _____

**7** Zoe partitions 4.768 into $\frac{47}{10}$ and $\frac{68}{1000}$. Write **two** other ways to partition 4.768.

**a.** _____

**b.** _____

**8** **a.** Circle the third fastest time.

47.8 sec      48.02 sec      48.182 sec      47.784 sec      48.62 sec      47.905 sec

**b.** Circle the fourth longest length.

7.6m      7.107m      7m      7.09m      7.121m      7.25m

# Multiplying decimals

## Remember

When multiplying a decimal by a whole number, it is important to think about the place value of the decimal.

For example: $0.6 \times 4 =$

Remember $0.6 = 6 \div 10$
The calculation could be: $6 \div 10 \times 4 =$
Rearrange the calculation: $6 \times 4 \div 10 =$
$24 \div 10 = 2.4$

$0.06 \times 4 =$

Remember $0.06 = 6 \div 100$
The calculation could be: $6 \div 100 \times 4 =$
Rearrange the calculation: $6 \times 4 \div 100 =$
$24 \div 100 = 0.24$

## Practise

**(1)** Complete these multiplications.

**a.** $0.3 \times 8 =$ _____

**b.** $0.6 \times 3 =$ _____

**c.** $0.7 \times 3 =$ _____

**d.** $0.4 \times 8 =$ _____

**e.** $0.9 \times 5 =$ _____

**f.** $0.7 \times 7 =$ _____

**(2)** Complete these multiplications.

**a.** $0.02 \times 7 =$ _____

**b.** $0.04 \times 11 =$ _____

**c.** $0.06 \times 6 =$ _____

**d.** $0.03 \times 9 =$ _____

**e.** $0.09 \times 6 =$ _____

**f.** $0.05 \times 12 =$ _____

**g.** $0.08 \times 8 =$ _____

**h.** $0.07 \times 8 =$ _____

**(3)** Find the missing numbers.

**a.** $0.3 \times$ _____ $= 1.5$

**b.** _____ $\times 4 = 3.6$

**c.** $4.2 =$ _____ $\times 7$

**d.** $2 = 0.5 \times$ _____

**e.** $0.08 \times$ _____ $= 0.72$

**f.** _____ $\times 3 = 0.12$

**g.** $0.81 =$ _____ $\times 9$

**h.** $0.4 = 0.08 \times$ _____

**Extend**

**4** Find the missing digits in these calculations. One has been done for you.

**a.**

```
        4 . 2  6  8
    ×              7
    ─────────────────
        0 . 0 [5] 6
        0 . 4 [2]
        [1]. 4
        2   8
    ─────────────────
    [2] 9 .[8] 7  6
```

**b.**

```
        3 . 7  3  5
    ×              3
    ─────────────────
        0 .[ ][ ] 5
        0 . 0  9
        [ ]. 1
        [ ]
    ─────────────────
    [ ] 1 . 2 [ ] 5
```

**c.**

```
        5 . 1  7  4
    ×              6
    ─────────────────
        0 .[ ] 2 [ ]
        [ ]. 4 [ ]
        0 .[ ]
        3 [ ]
    ─────────────────
    3 [ ].[ ] 4 [ ]
```

**d.**

```
        4 . 9  0  7
    ×              7
    ─────────────────
        0 .[ ] 4 [ ]
        0 .[ ]
        [ ].[ ]
        2 [ ]
    ─────────────────
    3 [ ].[ ] 4 [ ]
```

 **Apply**

**5** Solve these problems.

**a.** A bag of flour has a mass of 0.75kg. Bharti buys three bags. What is the total mass of flour? _____

**b.** A book costs £8.45 and a teacher buys eight books. What is the total cost of the books? _____

**c.** A glass holds 0.466 litres. Penny fills seven glasses with water. How much water will it take to fill all seven glasses? _____

**d.** Zainab is putting six shelves up in her garage. Each shelf is 1.35 metres long. What is the total length of the shelving? _____

**e.** A cross-country course is 1.085km long. A race is made up of five laps. What is the total length of the race? _____

# Dividing decimals

## Remember

When dividing a number by a whole number, the answer can be a decimal.
For example: 63 ÷ 4 = 15.75

6 tens ÷ 4 = 1 ten r.2 tens. Exchange 2 tens for 20 ones.
23 ones ÷ 4 = 5 ones r.3 ones. Exchange 3 ones for 30 tenths.
Add a decimal point and 0 in the tenths column.
30 tenths ÷ 4 = 7 tenths r.2 tenths. Exchange 2 tenths for 20 hundredths.
20 hundredths ÷ 4 = 5 hundredths.

$$\begin{array}{r} 1\phantom{0}5\,.\,7\phantom{0}5 \\ 4\,\overline{)\,6\,{}^2 3\,.\,{}^3 0\,{}^2 0} \end{array}$$

 **Practise**

**1** Complete these divisions. Write the answers as decimals with one decimal place.

**a.** 50 ÷ 4 = _____

**b.** 71 ÷ 5 = _____

**c.** 69 ÷ 5 = _____

**d.** 97 ÷ 2 = _____

**2** Complete these divisions. Write the answers as decimals with two decimal places.

**a.** 49 ÷ 4 = _____

**b.** 34 ÷ 8 = _____

**c.** 81 ÷ 12 = _____

**d.** 98 ÷ 8 = _____

**3** Find the missing numbers.

**a.** _____ ÷ 5 = 18.4

**b.** 23 ÷ _____ = 5.75

**c.** _____ ÷ 8 = 34.25

**d.** _____ ÷ 6 = 34.5

**4** Write these fractions as decimals.

**a.** $\frac{3}{5}$ = _____

**b.** $\frac{1}{4}$ = _____

**c.** $\frac{4}{5}$ = _____

**d.** $\frac{7}{20}$ = _____

**e.** $\frac{1}{25}$ = _____

**f.** $\frac{1}{8}$ = _____

**Tip** To change a fraction into a decimal, divide the numerator by the denominator. For example: $\frac{3}{4}$ = 3 ÷ 4 = 0.75

$$\begin{array}{r} 0\,.\,7\phantom{0}5 \\ 4\,\overline{)\,3\,.\,{}^3 0\,{}^2 0} \end{array}$$

**5** Here are five number cards.
Choose **three** cards to complete
the divisions.

2   3   4   5   6

a. ☐☐ ÷ ☐ = 8.6

b. ☐☐ ÷ ☐ = 15.5

c. ☐☐ ÷ ☐ = 8.4

d. ☐☐ ÷ ☐ = 22.5

**Tip** Try inverse operations using the answers and number cards to find the missing digits.

**6** Find the missing digits in these calculations.

a.
```
     1 ☐ . 8
   ┌─────────
 5 │ ☐³4 .⁴0
```

b.
```
      1 ☐ . 4 ☐
   ┌──────────────
 4 │ ☐³3 .¹8  8
```

c.
```
     ☐ . 4 ☐
   ┌──────────
 8 │ 5 1 . ☐²4
```

d.
```
      1 ☐ . ☐ ☐
   ┌──────────────
 6 │ ☐²9 .⁵5 ¹8
```

 **Apply**

**7** Solve these problems. Give your answers as decimals.

a. Four friends decide to share the cost of a meal equally.
The meal costs £77. How much does each friend pay?

_____

b. Mandy has 10 metres of ribbon to wrap 8 equally sized
presents. How much ribbon does she use for each present?

_____

c. Ying fills a 126-litre fish tank with buckets of water.
She uses 12 full buckets. How many litres of water
does the bucket hold?

_____

d. Luke cycles to and from work on 4 days one week.
Altogether, he cycles 142km. How long is each journey
in kilometres?

_____

e. A farmer has 410kg of potatoes, which she uses to fill 20
sacks with equal quantities. What is the mass of potatoes
in each sack?

_____

# Fractions, decimals and percentages

## Practise

**(1)** Write these fractions as decimals and percentages.

a. $\frac{4}{5}$ = _____ = _____

b. $\frac{17}{50}$ = _____ = _____

c. $\frac{13}{20}$ = _____ = _____

d. $\frac{17}{25}$ = _____ = _____

e. $\frac{9}{10}$ = _____ = _____

f. $\frac{1}{2}$ = _____ = _____

**(2)** Write these decimals as percentages and fractions in their simplest terms.

a. 0.15 = _____ = _____

b. 0.24 = _____ = _____

c. 0.46 = _____ = _____

d. 0.99 = _____ = _____

e. 0.7 = _____ = _____

f. 0.08 = _____ = _____

**(3)** Write these percentages as decimals and fractions in their simplest terms.

a. 35% = _____ = _____

b. 16% = _____ = _____

c. 90% = _____ = _____

d. 78% = _____ = _____

e. 5% = _____ = _____

f. 6% = _____ = _____

**Extend**

④ Write the correct symbol (<, > or =) in the circle to compare the fractions, decimals and percentages.

a. $\frac{1}{5}$ ◯ 0.18  b. 36% ◯ $\frac{7}{20}$  c. 0.4 ◯ 38%

d. $\frac{3}{10}$ ◯ 0.31  e. 73% ◯ $\frac{3}{4}$  f. $\frac{1}{20}$ ◯ 5%

> **Tip** Change fractions, decimals and percentages so that they are all the same (all either fractions, decimals or percentages) before comparing them.

⑤ Circle any fraction, decimal or percentage that is equal to four-fifths.

45%　　$\frac{8}{10}$　　0.45　　80%　　$\frac{40}{50}$　　0.8

⑥ Circle any fraction, decimal or percentage that is equal to sixty per cent.

$\frac{30}{50}$　　0.6　　6%　　$\frac{12}{20}$　　60.0%　　0.60

⑦ Write these fractions, decimals and percentages in order from smallest to largest.

55%　　0.6　　$\frac{13}{20}$　　0.45　　$\frac{6}{12}$

---

 **Apply**

⑧ Solve these problems.

a. Molly and Laurie complete two different tests. They each get a percentage score. Molly gets 17 out of 20 correct. Laurie gets 21 out of 25 correct. What is the difference between the two scores as a percentage? _____

b. A fuel gauge shows that the tank is 0.56 full. What fraction of the tank is empty? _____

c. Jenny and Omar have the same homework. Jenny has finished 72% and Omar has finished 80%. What is the difference between the amounts they have finished as a fraction? _____

d. Jason and Sara are collecting money for new school laptops. Jason has collected 15% of the total and Sara has collected 11%. What fraction of the total is still to be collected? _____

# Fractions word problems

 **Practise**

1. Solve these problems.

   **a.** There are red, blue and yellow counters in a jar. $\frac{2}{3}$ of the counters are red and $\frac{1}{5}$ are blue. What fraction of the counters are yellow? _____

   **Tip** Remember that all the counters in the jar together will represent one whole or 1.

   **b.** On a walk, Freddie has walked $3\frac{4}{5}$ km and Malik has walked $5\frac{1}{10}$ km.

   **i.** How much further has Malik walked than Freddie? Give your answer as a mixed number. _____

   **ii.** Round this mixed number to the nearest whole kilometre. _____

   **c.** Barry completes a maths practice test. He gets 17 out of 20 questions correct. The teacher writes his score as a percentage. What is the percentage? _____

   **d.** Naomi has some homework to do. She works for $\frac{3}{4}$ of an hour on Friday, $1\frac{1}{2}$ hours on Saturday and $\frac{5}{12}$ of an hour on Sunday. How long does she spend on her homework altogether? Give your answer as a mixed number. _____

   **e.** A £1 coin has a thickness of 3.15mm and a mass of 9.5g.

   **i.** How high will a pile of nine £1 coins be? _____

   **ii.** Round this height to the nearest millimetre. _____

   **iii.** What is the mass of nine £1 coins? _____

   **iv.** Round this mass to the nearest g. _____

**Extend**

**2** Solve these problems.

**a.** In a jar of counters, $\frac{2}{3}$ of the counters are red and $\frac{1}{5}$ are blue. What fraction gives the difference between red and blue counters? _____

**b.** A two-litre bottle of lemonade has 1500ml left. 4 friends share the remaining drink equally. What fraction of the bottle do they each drink? _____

**c.** A teacher buys a set of 6 books that cost £12.45 each and a set of 8 books that cost £9.55 each. If he had £200 to spend, how much will he have left? _____

**d.** This is a fuel gauge. How full is the tank? Write the answer as a fraction, decimal and percentage.

_____

**Apply**

**3** Solve these problems.

**a.** In a jar of counters, $\frac{2}{3}$ of the counters are red. $\frac{2}{5}$ of the red counters are large. What fraction of all the counters are large, red counters? _____

**b.** Matt and George complete fifty one-mark questions. Matt gets 35 questions right. George scored 8% more than Matt. How many questions did George get right? _____

**c.** James earns £327 for a job. He pays 20% of his earnings in tax.

  **i.** How much does he have left? _____

  **ii.** He spends $\frac{3}{8}$ of the money he has after tax. How much does he have left? _____

  **iii.** Round the amount he has left to the nearest pound. _____

**d.** Hannah scores 13 out of 20 in a spelling test. Mya scores 17 out of 25 in a different spelling test. Their marks are given as a percentage. How much higher was Mya's percentage than Hannah's? _____

**e.** A jar has 500 red, blue and yellow counters. Some counters are small and some are large. $\frac{7}{25}$ of the counters are red and 30% of the red counters are small. How many large, red counters are there? _____

# Ratio

## Remember

Ratio compares two or more amounts with each other. For example: 3 parts compared to 5 parts. This is written using a colon as $3:5$ (said '3 to 5'). In the same way as fractions, ratios have equivalents. For example: ratios of $6:10$ parts and $9:15$ parts are both equivalent to a ratio of $3:5$. Ratios can compare more than two amounts. For example: 3 parts compared to 5 parts compared to 12 parts. This is written as $3:5:12$. In the ratio $3:5$, the total is found by adding the parts in the ratio: $3 + 5 = 8$. The 3 represents $\frac{3}{8}$ of the total and the 5 represents $\frac{5}{8}$ of the total.

## Practise

**1** Fill in the missing numbers in the sentences using these counters.

   **a.** For every five shaded counters, there are _____ unshaded counters.

   **b.** For every three unshaded counters, there are _____ counters in total.

   **c.** For every eight counters, there are _____ shaded counters.

**2** Fill in the missing numbers in the sentences using these triangles.

   **a.** For every three unshaded triangles, there are _____ shaded triangles.

   **b.** For every seven shaded triangles, there are _____ triangles in total.

   **c.** For every ten triangles, there are _____ unshaded triangles.

**3** There are 4 black squares for every 6 white squares. Fill in the missing numbers in the sentences.

   **a.** For every three white squares, there are _____ black squares.

   **b.** For every twenty black squares, there are _____ squares in total.

   **c.** For every thirty squares, there are _____ white squares.

   **d.** For every twelve black squares, there are _____ white squares.

# Extend

**4** Here are some shapes. Write these ratios using the shapes.

a. The ratio of squares to other shapes is _____ : _____.

b. The ratio of triangles to other shapes is _____ : _____.

c. The ratio of squares to circles to triangles is _____ : _____ : _____.

**5** Simplify these ratios.

a. 16:4 _____ : _____        b. 16:24 _____ : _____

c. 8:12 _____ : _____        d. 15:25 _____ : _____

**6** In the ratio 2:5, one amount is 10. What is the other amount? Give **two** possible answers.

a. _____        b. _____

# Apply

**7** Solve these problems.

a. When training, Zoe runs 4 laps for every 3 laps that she jogs.

　　i. If she runs for 12 laps, how many laps does she jog? _____

　　ii. If she jogs for 12 laps, how many laps does she run? _____

b. Owen earns £25 for every 3 cars he washes.

　　i. If Owen earns £100, how many cars does he wash? _____

　　ii. If Owen washes 9 cars, how much money does he earn? _____

c. Olivia has a collection of books. 35 are fiction books and 25 are non-fiction books. What is the ratio of fiction books to non-fiction books in its simplest form? _____

d. A recipe for a drink uses orange juice, lemon juice and lemonade in the ratio of 4:1:3

　　i. If 200ml of orange juice is used, how much lemonade is used? _____

　　ii. If 900ml of lemonade is used, how much lemon juice is used? _____

　　iii. If 480ml of lemonade is used, how much drink is made? _____

# Proportion

## Practise

**(1)** Write these proportions as fractions. Simplify the fractions where necessary.

   **a.** 5 out of 12 = _____    **b.** 9 out of 10 = _____    **c.** 8 out of 20 = _____

   **d.** 30 out of 100 = _____    **e.** 26 out of 50 = _____    **f.** 18 out of 48 = _____

   **g.** 10 out of 45 = _____    **h.** 24 out of 36 = _____    **i.** 150 out of 200 = _____

**Tip**  You can simplify a proportion by finding a common factor of both numbers.

**(2)** Find the missing numbers in these sets of equivalent proportions.

   **a.** 7 out of 8 = 21 out of _____ = _____ out of 40 = 70 out of _____

   **b.** 3 out of 4 = 15 out of _____ = _____ out of 28 = 36 out of _____

   **c.** _____ out of 6 = 20 out of _____ = 30 out of 36 = 45 out of _____

   **d.** _____ out of 9 = 24 out of _____ = 40 out of 45 = 64 out of _____

**(3)** Solve these problems.

   **a.** If 6 boxes have a mass of 42kg, what is the mass of 12 boxes?    _____

   **b.** If 5 boxes hold 40 toys, how many toys are held in 15 boxes?    _____

   **c.** If 3 boxes have a volume of 1200cm³, what is the volume of 9 boxes?    _____

   **d.** If 8 boxes have a capacity of 2400ml, what is the capacity of 9 boxes?    _____

   **e.** If there are 144 eggs in 12 boxes, how many eggs are in 7 boxes?    _____

   **f.** If 10 boxes have a volume of 3.6 litres, what is the volume of 3 boxes?    _____

## ⫸ Extend

**4** Mia is making party bags. These are the items she buys for the party bags. Each party bag must have 1 of each item. If there are 24 children, how much must Mia spend to make party bags for all the children?

_____

**Price list:**

| | |
|---|---|
| Puzzles | £2.75 for 6 |
| Pencils | £1.40 for 12 |
| Bubble blowers | £1.20 for 2 |
| Mini games | £3.40 for 8 |

**5** This is the recipe for a fruit drink.

  **a.** How much pineapple juice is needed for 6 people? _____

  **b.** How many lemons are needed for 30 people? _____

  **c.** How much orange juice is needed for 18 people? _____

  **d.** If 2 oranges are used, how much lemonade is used? _____

  **e.** How many people will a fruit drink using 2 litres of orange juice serve? _____

  **f.** How many strawberries are needed for 18 people? _____

**Fruit drink (serves 3 people)**

10 strawberries

$\frac{1}{2}$ orange

$\frac{1}{2}$ lemon

500ml pineapple juice

400ml orange juice

300ml lemonade

## ☁ Apply

**6** Solve these problems.

  **a.** Bananas cost £1.20 per kg. What is the cost of 600g of bananas? _____

  **b.** Two parcels have a mass of 3kg. One parcel is three times the mass of the other? What are the masses of each parcel? _____ and _____

  **c.** Copper pipe costs £32 for 10 metres. What is the cost of 6 metres? _____

  **d.** Bags of nails are priced by mass. Sam spends £2.40 on a bag of nails with a mass of 250g.

  **i.** How much do the nails cost per 100g? _____

  **ii.** If Sam spends £1.80 on a bag of nails, what is the mass of the nails? _____

  **e.** A row of 12 tiles is 1.92 metres long.

  **i.** What is the length of 30 tiles? _____

  **ii.** How many tiles are there in 3.2 metres? _____

# Unequal sharing

Extend

## Remember

Sharing or dividing usually groups numbers or quantities into equal amounts. Using a ratio or proportion can divide a number or quantity into unequal amounts.

For example: using a ratio

Divide £30 in the ratio of 3:2          This ratio has 5 shares (3 + 2).
30 ÷ 5 = 6                              Each share has a value of 6.
6 × 3 = 18 and 6 × 2 = 12              The two parts are £18 and £12.

For example: using a proportion

Jo spends £2 out of every £3 on food.
Altogether, Jo spent £24 on food. How much money did Jo have?
24 ÷ 2 = 12
12 × 3 = 36                            Jo had £36.

## Practise

**1** Solve these ratio calculations.

**a.** Divide 75 in the ratio 3:2.

_____ and _____

**b.** Divide 120 in the ratio 2:1.

_____ and _____

**c.** Divide 300 in the ratio 1:4.

_____ and _____

**d.** Divide 160 in the ratio 3:5.

_____ and _____

**e.** Divide 91 in the ratio 3:4.

_____ and _____

**f.** Divide 144 in the ratio 5:1.

_____ and _____

**2** Abi has a set of cards. For every 12 cards, 9 of the cards are in colour and the rest are in black and white.

**a.** How many cards are in colour if she has 60 cards?          _____

**b.** How many cards are in colour if she has 144 cards?          _____

**c.** How many cards are there if 36 are in colour?          _____

**d.** How many cards are there if 72 are in colour?          _____

**e.** How many cards are there if 36 are **not** in colour?          _____

**f.** How many cards are there if 15 are **not** in colour?          _____

# Extend

**3** Complete the table.

| | Ratio | Total amount | Larger amount | Smaller amount |
|---|---|---|---|---|
| **a.** | 3:2 | 60 | | |
| **b.** | : | | 18 | 12 |
| **c.** | :1 | 36 | 30 | |
| **d.** | 5: | 14 | 10 | |

**4** Complete the table.

| | Proportion | Total | Part given | Part remaining |
|---|---|---|---|---|
| **a.** | 3 out of every 4 | | 9 | |
| **b.** | 2 out of every 5 | 25 | | |
| **c.** | out of every 5 | 20 | 16 | |
| **d.** | 3 out of every | 16 | | 4 |

# Apply

**5** Solve these problems.

**a.** Potatoes cost 40p per kg. How much would 2.5kg of potatoes cost? _____

**b.** 5ml of plant food is mixed with 2 litres of water. Pat has a 25ml bottle of plant food. How much water will it be mixed with? _____

**c.** The school prepares sandwiches for a picnic. The sandwiches are either tuna or cheese. 3 out of every 5 sandwiches are tuna and there are 24 tuna sandwiches.

  **i.** How many sandwiches are there in total? _____

  **ii.** What is the ratio of tuna sandwiches to cheese sandwiches? _____

  **iii.** What fraction of the sandwiches are cheese sandwiches? _____

# Finding percentages

## Remember

Percentages are a type of fraction that show an amount or quantity as a fraction out of one hundred, that is as hundredths. For example: 55% = 55 out of 100 = $\frac{55}{100}$ = $\frac{11}{20}$.
55% can also be written as the decimal 0.55. There are several different methods that can be used to find a percentage of a number.

For example: Find 30% of 80.

**Using fractions**
30% = $\frac{30}{100}$
Find $\frac{30}{100}$ of 80.
$\qquad$ 80 ÷ 100 = 0.8
$\qquad$ 0.8 × 30 = 24

**Using the '10% method'**
10% = $\frac{10}{100}$ = $\frac{1}{10}$
Find $\frac{1}{10}$ of 80.
$\qquad$ 80 ÷ 10 = 8
30% of 80 = 8 × 3 = 24

**Using decimals**
30% = 0.3
80 × 0.3 = 24

The answer is 24.

## Practise

**1** Write these fractions and decimals as percentages.

**a.** $\frac{9}{10}$ = _____

**b.** 0.23 = _____

**c.** $\frac{1}{20}$ = _____

**d.** 0.83 = _____

**e.** $\frac{25}{50}$ = _____

**f.** 0.09 = _____

**2** Write the correct symbol (<, > or =) in the circle to compare the fractions, decimals and percentages.

**a.** $\frac{7}{10}$ ◯ 0.69 ◯ 68%

**b.** 40% ◯ $\frac{2}{5}$ ◯ 0.4

**c.** 0.07 ◯ $\frac{4}{50}$ ◯ 9%

**d.** $\frac{9}{50}$ ◯ 19% ◯ 0.2

**3** Find these percentages.

**a.** 20% of 80 = _____

**b.** 40% of 120 = _____

**c.** 50% of 65 = _____

**d.** 80% of 90 = _____

**e.** 25% of 180 = _____

**f.** 75% of 300 = _____

**g.** 30% of 300 = _____

**h.** 99% of 900 = _____

**i.** 70% of 140 = _____

**j.** 30% of 15 = _____

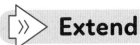

## Extend

4. Find the missing number.

   **a.** 25% of _____ = 15

   **b.** 20% of _____ = 5

   **c.** 10% of _____ = 35

   **d.** 70% of _____ = 35

   **e.** 75% of _____ = 45

   **f.** 20% of _____ = 100

5. Write the correct symbol (<, > or =) in the circle to compare the numbers.

   **a.** 30% of 40 $\bigcirc$ 40% of 30

   **b.** 25% of 240 $\bigcirc$ 70% of 90

   **c.** 75% of 360 $\bigcirc$ 90% of 300

   **d.** 5% of 800 $\bigcirc$ 70% of 50

   **e.** 20% of 450 $\bigcirc$ 75% of 120

   **f.** 5% of 1000 $\bigcirc$ 60% of 150

## Apply

6. Solve these problems.

   **a.** Ed has 40 one-mark questions for homework and has completed 80%. How many questions does he have left to do?

   **b.** Nia gets 10 questions correct in a quiz. In the next quiz, she improves her score by 100%. How many questions does she get right in the next quiz?

   **c.** In a primary school, 15% of the children are in Year 6. There are 30 children in Year 6. How many children are in the primary school?

   **d.** There is a delivery of 1600 cans of drink at a supermarket. 70% are cans of cola and of these cans of cola, 15% are cans of diet cola. How many cans of diet cola are delivered?

   **e.** Suzie did a test with 20 questions and got a score of 80% while Scott did a test with 30 similar questions and got a score of 70%. How many more questions did Scott get right than Suzie?

   **f.** Sanjit checks the photos on his phone. There are 776 photos and 75% of them include him. How many photos show Sanjit?

# Scale factors

## Remember

Shapes that are the same size but have been rotated or reflected are known as congruent shapes. These shapes are congruent.

Shapes that look the same but have different sizes are known as similar shapes. These shapes are similar. They have been enlarged.

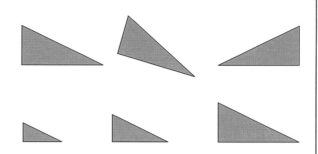

A scale gives the ratio of two measurements of similar shapes. A scale factor shows what the lengths of one shape have been multiplied by to make a similar shape.

For example: The lengths of a triangle are 4cm, 7cm and 9cm. If the lengths are increased by a scale factor of 3, they will become 12cm, 21cm and 27cm.

## Practise

(1) Here are two similar quadrilaterals. Quadrilateral A has been increased by a scale factor of 3 to make Quadrilateral B. Write the missing measurements on the quadrilaterals.

15cm

_____ cm

A

_____ cm

18cm

_____ cm

42cm

36cm

B

_____ cm

(2) Complete this table showing the measurements of a triangle.

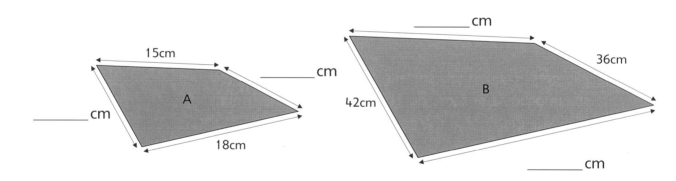

|   |   | Triangle E | | Triangle F |
|---|---|---|---|---|
| a. | Side 1 | 6.5cm | | |
| b. | Side 2 | | is increased by a scale factor of 5 | 25.5cm |
| c. | Side 3 | 3.3cm | | |

Unit 4 • Ratio and proportion

Schofield & Sims

**3** These triangles are all similar. Find the missing measurements.

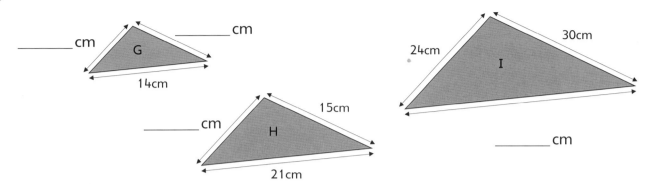

**4** The measurements of a triangle are 15cm, 18cm and 25cm. The triangle is enlarged by a scale factor of 4. What are the new measurements?

_____ , _____ and _____

**5** The measurements of a triangle are 20cm, 28cm and 32cm. The triangle is enlarged. The new measurements are 50cm, 70cm and 80cm. What scale factor is used? _____

## Apply

**6** Solve these problems.

**a.** Harry draws a plan of his back garden. It is a rectangle 15cm long and 10cm wide. In real life, the garden is 15m long and 10m wide. What is the scale used for the plan?   1 : _____

**b.** Lucy draws a design of squares and rectangles. The squares have sides of 3cm. The rectangles are 6cm long and 3cm wide. She arranges them in this way:

Lucy repeats the design to make a final pattern that is 60cm long.

**i.** How many squares will be in the final pattern? _____

**ii.** How many rectangles will be in the final pattern? _____

**c.** Yusuf wants to draw a plan of a house that is 14m long and 7m wide. To fit the plan on the paper, Yusuf needs to use a scale factor of $\frac{1}{50}$. What will the length and width of the house be on the plan?

_____ and _____

**Tip** Similar shapes are enlarged when the scale factor is greater than 1 and become smaller when the scale factor is between 0 and 1.

# Algebraic expressions

## Remember

Algebra uses symbols and letters to stand for numbers. These symbols or letters may be unknowns or variables.

An unknown can be worked out.

For example:
6 + ⬤ = 7
⬤ must equal 1.

A variable could have any value.

For example:
6 + ⬤ + ◾ = 20
⬤ or ◾ could equal any number.

$$3n + 5 = 16$$

| | | |
|---|---|---|
| 3n, 5 and 16 are terms. A number, an unknown or a variable is a term. | 3n + 5 is an expression. Terms are joined with an operator. +, −, × and ÷ are operators. | 3n + 5 = 16 is an equation. A number statement showing terms or expressions equal each other is an equation. |

## Practise

**(1)** Write these statements as expressions.

**a.** 5 more than $a$ _____

**b.** 4 added to $e$ _____

**c.** 7 subtracted from $f$ _____

**d.** $h$ minus 9 _____

**e.** $i$ multiplied by 6 _____

**f.** 8 multiplied by $j$ _____

**g.** $k$ divided by 4 _____

**h.** 10 divided by $l$ _____

**Tip** In algebra, multiplication is written without a multiplication sign. The number is written before the symbol, so $5 × n = 5n$. Division is usually written as a fraction, so $12 ÷ n = \frac{12}{n}$ and $n ÷ 12 = \frac{n}{12}$.

**(2)** **a.** Circle the simplified form of the expression $5n + 7n − 2$. Circle **one**.

$14n$ $\qquad$ $10n$ $\qquad$ $12n − 2$ $\qquad$ $2n + 10$ $\qquad$ $2n + 14$

**b.** Circle the simplified form of the expression $7n + 8 − 3n$. Circle **one**.

$12 + 2n$ $\qquad$ $4n + 8$ $\qquad$ $10n + 8$ $\qquad$ $18n + 8$ $\qquad$ $13n$

**3** Here are one-step function machines. Write each function machine as an algebraic expression.

| Input | 1st operation | Algebraic expression |
|---|---|---|
| **a.** $m$ | + 7 | |
| **b.** $n$ | ÷ 3 | |

| Input | 1st operation | Algebraic expression |
|---|---|---|
| **c.** $p$ | × 5 | |
| **d.** $q$ | − 8 | |

**4** Here are two-step function machines. Write each function machine as an algebraic expression.

| Input | 1st operation | 2nd operation | Algebraic expression |
|---|---|---|---|
| **a.** $r$ | × 4 | − 6 | |
| **b.** $t$ | ÷ 2 | + 4 | |
| **c.** $u$ | − 6 | ÷ 5 | |
| **d.** $v$ | × 5 | + 3 | |

**5** **a.** Find the value of the expression $5x + 6$ if:

    **i.** $x = 4$ _____           **ii.** $x = 12$ _____

  **b.** If the value of the expression $5x + 6$ is 21, what is the value of $x$? _____

 **Apply**

**6** Oliver has some pocket money saved. Write an algebraic expression for the money Oliver has after each of these calculations. Use the term $x$ for Oliver's pocket money.

  **a.** Oliver spends £8 of his pocket money on cards. _____

  **b.** Oliver spends $\frac{1}{2}$ of his pocket money on a T-shirt. _____

  **c.** Oliver gets £20 as a birthday present. _____

  **d.** Oliver saves all the money he can and doubles the amount of pocket money he has saved. _____

  **e.** Oliver spends $\frac{1}{8}$ of his pocket money but then is given another £5. _____

# Unknowns

Extend

## Remember

An unknown is a letter or a symbol that is used in an equation. It can be worked out because there is only one possible solution. For example: $6 + n = 15$. There is only one number that can be added to 6 to give 15 as an answer. $15 - 6 = 9$. The unknown, $n$, must be 9: $6 + 9 = 15$

Some equations may have two unknowns. For example: $a + b = 15$ where $a$ and $b$ are consecutive numbers. There are many combinations of two numbers totalling 15:

$14 + 1 = 15$        $14.9 + 0.1 = 15$        $-1 + 16 = 15$

But there are only two consecutive numbers that total 15 and they are 7 and 8.

## Practise

**(1)** Find the missing numbers.

   **a.** $32 - \blacksquare = 17$     $\blacksquare =$ _____     **b.** $4\bullet = 36$     $\bullet =$ _____

   **c.** $\dfrac{\bullet}{6} = 8$     $\bullet =$ _____     **d.** $\dfrac{48}{\blacksquare} = 8$     $\blacksquare =$ _____

   **e.** $\blacksquare + \dfrac{1}{2} = 6$     $\blacksquare =$ _____     **f.** $\bullet - 18 = 23$     $\bullet =$ _____

**(2)** Find the missing numbers. The totals for the columns and rows are shown. One has been done for you.

**a.**

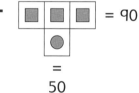

$\blacksquare = \underline{\ 30\ }$     $\bullet = \underline{\ 20\ }$

**b.**

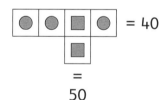

$\blacksquare =$ _____     $\bullet =$ _____

**c.**

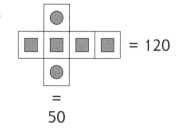

$\blacksquare =$ _____     $\bullet =$ _____

**d.**

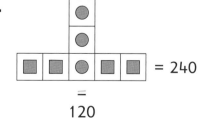

$\blacksquare =$ _____     $\bullet =$ _____

# Extend

**3** Find the missing positive whole numbers.

**a.** $a$ is half the value of $b$.

$a + 2b = 10$

$a =$ _____  $b =$ _____

**b.** $c$ is twice the value of $d$.

$2c + d = 50$

$c =$ _____  $d =$ _____

**c.** $f$ is three times the value of $e$.

$2e + f = 25$

$e =$ _____  $f =$ _____

**d.** $g$ is four times the value of $h$.

$4g + h = 34$

$g =$ _____  $h =$ _____

**4** Find the missing positive whole numbers.

**a.** $a + b = 12$ and $a - b = 8$

$a =$ _____  $b =$ _____

**b.** $c + d = 20$ and $c - d = 10$

$c =$ _____  $d =$ _____

**c.** $e \times f = 48$ and $e \div f = 3$

$e =$ _____  $f =$ _____

**d.** $g \times h = 60$ and $g \div h = 60$

$g =$ _____  $h =$ _____

# Apply

**5** Solve these problems.

**a.** A cup of coffee costs 40p more than a cup of tea. Sally buys three cups of coffee and a cup of tea for £11.60.

   **i.** How much does a cup of coffee cost? _____

   **ii.** How much does a cup of tea cost? _____

**b.** This bar is divided into rectangles of two sizes, Rectangle A and Rectangle B. Rectangle A is twice the length of Rectangle B.

| 42cm | | | |
|---|---|---|---|
| A | A | A | B |

What are the lengths of Rectangle A and Rectangle B?

Rectangle A is _____ cm and Rectangle B is _____ cm.

**c.** Rishi buys two different types of books. The maths books cost £8 each, which is £3 more than the reading books. He buys 6 books and spends £42 altogether. How many reading books and how many maths books does Rishi buy?

_____ maths books and _____ reading books

# Variables

## Remember

A variable is a letter or a symbol that is used in an expression or an equation. It may be possible to work out the value of the variable, but there may also be a number of possible solutions.

For example: $a + b = 15$. There are many answers. $0 + 15 = 15$, $0.5 + 14.5 = 15$, $7\frac{1}{3} + 7\frac{2}{3} = 15$, $-5 + 20 = 15$ and so on. If you are given extra information, for example that $a$ and $b$ are both positive multiples of 5, then there are a limited number of answers. $5 + 10 = 15$ and $10 + 5 = 15$

## Practise

**(1)** These shapes represent different positive whole numbers. What could the values of the shapes be? Give **one** solution for each.

**a.** ● + ● + ■ = 9          ● = _____     ■ = _____

**b.** ▲ + ▲ + ▲ + ◆ = 11          ▲ = _____     ◆ = _____

**Tip** Decide what one of the shapes could be, then see if the second value is possible.

**(2)** These letters represent different positive whole numbers. What could the values of the letters be? Give **three** solutions for each.

**a.** A + B + B + B = 16

A = _____  B = _____

A = _____  B = _____

A = _____  B = _____

**b.** C + C + D + D + D = 23

C = _____  D = _____

C = _____  D = _____

C = _____  D = _____

**(3)** These letters represent different positive whole numbers. What could the values of the letters be? Give **three** solutions for each.

**a.** $ef = 48$

e = _____  f = _____

e = _____  f = _____

e = _____  f = _____

**b.** $gh = 36$

g = _____  h = _____

g = _____  h = _____

g = _____  h = _____

# Extend

**4** These letters represent different positive whole numbers. What could the values of the letters be? Give **one** solution for each.

**a.** $j + 4 = k - 5$    $j =$ _____    $k =$ _____

**b.** $m + 5 = n + 7$    $m =$ _____    $n =$ _____

**c.** $p + 5 = qr$    $p =$ _____    $q =$ _____    $r =$ _____

**d.** $st = uv$    $s =$ _____    $t =$ _____    $u =$ _____    $v =$ _____

**5** The letters are different positive whole numbers. What could the values of the letters be? Give **three** solutions for each.

**a.** $2w + x = 12$

    $w =$ _____    $x =$ _____

    $w =$ _____    $x =$ _____

    $w =$ _____    $x =$ _____

**b.** $y + 4z = 17$

    $y =$ _____    $z =$ _____

    $y =$ _____    $z =$ _____

    $y =$ _____    $z =$ _____

# Apply

**6** Solve these problems.

**a.** Samir is under 40 years old. Max is over 10 years old. If Samir is three times older than Max, how old is Samir? Give **one** answer. _____

**b.** Jo has three different coins. The coins could be 5p, 10p, 20p or 50p coins. Write the **four** amounts Jo could have.

    _____ , _____ , _____ or _____

**c.** Jack spends £15. He buys both coffee and tea. A coffee costs £3 and a tea costs £2. How many cups of coffee and of tea could Jack have bought? Give **two** answers.

    **i.** _____

    **ii.** _____

**d.** Megan collects 54 eggs from her hens. She puts all the eggs into boxes of 6 or 12 eggs. How many boxes of 6 and of 12 could she have filled? Give **two** answers.

    **i.** _____

    **ii.** _____

# Formulae and linear sequences

## Remember

A formula is a set of instructions for solving a problem. The instructions are written using numbers, letters and operators.

For example: To find the perimeter of a rectangle, add the length and width and double the total. This can be shortened to $P = 2(L + W)$ where $P$ is the perimeter, $L$ is the length and $W$ is the width.

Formulae can also be used to find a number in a sequence.

For example: A formula for an 'add 6' sequence is $6n$ where $n$ is the position in the sequence of the number that you want to find. The third multiple of 6 ($6n$) is $6 \times 3 = 18$. An 'add 6' sequence that begins with 5 (which is 1 less than 6) is $6n - 1$. The third number in this sequence is $6 \times 3 - 1 = 17$.

## Practise

**(1)** Use these formulae.

  **a.** The perimeter of a rectangle is given by the formula $P = 2(L + W)$.

  Find the perimeter of a rectangle if the length ($L$) is 15cm and the width ($W$) is 12cm. _____

  **b.** The perimeter of a regular octagon is given by the formula $P = 8L$.

  Find the perimeter of a regular octagon if the length ($L$) is 15cm. _____

  **c.** The area of a rectangle is given by the formula $A = L \times W$.

  Find the area of a rectangle if the length ($L$) is 25cm and the width ($W$) is 9cm. _____

  **d.** The diameter of a circle is given by the formula $D = 2R$.

  Find the diameter of a circle if the radius ($R$) is 12.25cm. _____

  **e.** The area of a triangle is given by the formula $A = \frac{1}{2}(B \times H)$.

  Find the area of a triangle if the base ($B$) is 12cm and the height ($H$) is 7cm. _____

**(2)** Use these formulae to find the 4th term (number) in each sequence.

  **a.** $5n + 2$ _____    **b.** $3n - 1$ _____    **c.** $6n + 3$ _____

**3** Here is a sequence:   4        10        16        22        28

    **a.** Circle the formula that describes the sequence.

        $4n + 6$        $4n + 2$        $6n + 4$        $6n - 2$        $10n - 6$

    **b.** Use the chosen formula to find the 12th term in the sequence.   _____

**4** Here is a sequence:   9        13        17        21        25

    **a.** Circle the formula that describes the sequence.

        $4n + 1$        $4n + 5$        $n + 9$        $3n - 2$        $9n + 4$

    **b.** Use the chosen formula to find the 20th term in the sequence.   _____

## Apply

**5** Solve these problems.

    **a.** Jay uses the formula, $7n - 2$, to write a sequence of numbers. Jay says that the 15th number of the sequence is 102. Is Jay correct? Explain your answer.

    _____

    **b.** Leah makes sandwiches for buffets. She uses the formula $C = S(0.45 + 0.15)$ to work out the cost, where $C$ is the total cost and $S$ is the number of sandwiches. For each sandwich, the filling costs £0.45 and the bread costs £0.15.

        **i.** Find the cost of 40 sandwiches.   _____

        **ii.** Find the cost of 120 sandwiches.   _____

        **iii.** How many sandwiches would Leah make for £240?   _____

    **c.** This table shows the output numbers of a two-step function machine.

| Term | Output |
|------|--------|
| 1st | 12 |
| 2nd | 16 |
| 3rd | 20 |

        **i.** What is the formula for the sequence?

        _____

        **ii.** What is the 25th term in the sequence?

        _____

# Units of measurement

## Remember

Metric units of measure are used for length, mass and capacity.

**Length:** 10mm = 1 cm, 100cm = 1m, 1000m = 1km

**Mass:** 1000g = 1 kilogram     **Capacity:** 100cl = 1l, 1000ml = 1 litre

## Practise

(1) Convert these units of measurement.

    **a.** 10.5m = _____ cm      **b.** 10.5kg = _____ g

    **c.** 1.005 litres = _____ ml      **d.** 1000mm = _____ cm

    **e.** 7095ml = _____ litres      **f.** 9.06km = _____ m

(2) Write these measurements in order from shortest to longest.

    5000mm     5.5m     505cm     5.55m     500mm

_____

(3) Write these measurements in order from heaviest to lightest.

    5.5kg     5050g     5.005kg     5kg     5055g

_____

(4) Write these measurements in order from least to most.

    $\frac{1}{2}$ litre     0.55 litres     505ml     555ml     5 litres

_____

(5) Write the letter on the scale that corresponds to each of these lengths.

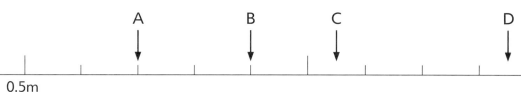

60cm = _____      925mm = _____      0.7m = _____      77.5cm = _____

# Extend

**6** Calculate:

**a.** 3m − 25cm = _____ cm

**b.** 2kg + 25g = _____ kg

**c.** 1.5 litres − 25ml = _____ litres

**d.** 45mm × 5 = _____ cm

**7** **a.** Complete these approximations using the approximation 5 miles ≈ 8km.

    **i.** 40 miles ≈ _____ km

    **ii.** 40km ≈ _____ miles

    **iii.** 100 miles ≈ _____ km

    **iv.** 12km ≈ _____ miles

**b.** If 2.5cm ≈ 1 inch, approximately how many centimetres are in 12 inches? _____

**c.** If 4.5 litres ≈ 1 gallon, approximately how many litres are in 8 gallons? _____

**8** Use the measurements in the box to write equivalents.

| 4000mm | 0.4km | 400m | 400cm |

> **Tip** Use the units to work out whether to multiply or divide and by how much. For example: 10mm = 1cm, so multiply by 10 when changing cm to mm.

**a.** _____ = _____

**b.** _____ = _____

# Apply

**9** Solve these problems.

**a.** A box contains 1.25kg of cereal. Keeley uses 50g of cereal each morning. How many days will the box of cereal last? _____

**b.** Potatoes cost £1.20 per kg.

    **i.** What is the cost of 300g of potatoes? _____

    **ii.** What mass of potatoes can be bought for 90p? _____

**c.** Three identical large parcels have a total mass of 2.4kg. Five identical small parcels have the same total mass. How much heavier is one large parcel than one small parcel? _____

**d.** A set of scales shows the mass of some flour is 1.35kg. Sanjay adds another 75g of flour to the scales. What mass do the scales now show? _____

**e.** Dean is 10mm taller than Nico, who is 3cm shorter than Chen. Chen is 1.51m tall. How tall is Dean? _____

# Perimeter and area

## Remember

Perimeter is the distance around the outside edge of a 2D shape. As it is a distance, it is measured in units of length. For example: mm, cm or m. To find the perimeter of a rectangle, use the formula: $P = 2(L + W)$, where $L$ = length and $W$ = width. Area is the amount of space taken up by a 2D shape. Area is measured in square units. For example: $mm^2$, $cm^2$ or $m^2$. To find the area of a rectangle, use the formula: $A = L \times W$, where $L$ = length and $W$ = width.

To find the area of a parallelogram, use the formula: $A = B \times H$, where $B$ = base and $H$ = height.

 Rearranging the parallelogram can make a rectangle with the same area.

To find the area of a triangle, use the formula: $\frac{1}{2}(B \times H)$, where $B$ = base and $H$ = height.

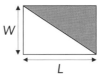 A triangle is half the size of a rectangle.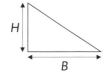

## Practise

(1) Calculate the perimeter and area of each shape. Write the answers in centimetres or square centimetres.

**a.** composite rectilinear hexagon

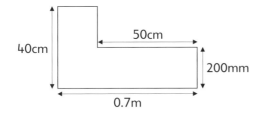

perimeter = _____ cm

area = _____ $cm^2$

**b.** acute-angled scalene triangle

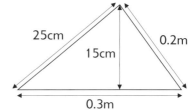

perimeter = _____ cm

area = _____ $cm^2$

**c.** parallelogram

perimeter = _____ cm

area = _____ $cm^2$

> **Tip** Calculate perimeters and areas using measurements in the same unit.

**2** This rectangle is made of square centimetre tiles. It has an area of 24cm². Rearrange the tiles to make **three** other rectangles with the same area.

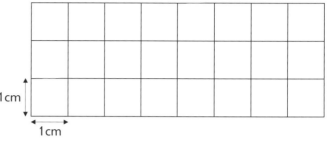

**a.** length = _____ width = _____

**b.** length = _____ width = _____

**c.** length = _____ width = _____

**3** A parallelogram and a triangle both have bases of 60cm and areas of 600cm².

**a.** What is the height of the parallelogram? _____

**b.** What is the height of the triangle? _____

 **Apply**

**4** Solve these problems. Write the units for each answer.

**a.** This shape is made of four regular hexagons.
The perimeter of each hexagon is 72cm.
What is the perimeter of the shape?

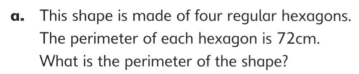

_____

**b.** Two rectangles each have lengths of 18cm and widths of 6cm.
One rectangle is placed on the other so they overlap as shown.

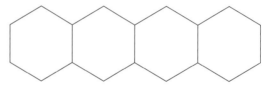

**i.** What is the perimeter of the new shape? _____

**ii.** What is the area of the new shape? _____

**c.** A square is 12cm long and 12cm wide. A rectangle is 6cm longer and 3cm narrower than the square.

**i.** What is the difference between the perimeters of the two shapes? _____

**ii.** What is the difference between the areas of the two shapes? _____

**d.** The perimeter of a rectangle is 120cm and the length is three times the width. What is the area of the rectangle? _____

**e.** The area of a square is 225cm². What is the perimeter of the square? _____

# Volume

## Remember

Volume is the amount of space taken up by a 3D shape. It is measured in cubic units, such as cubic centimetres (cm³) or cubic metres (m³).

This cuboid is 5cm long, 3cm wide and 2cm high.
There are 5 centimetre cubes in one row.
There are 3 rows of 5 centimetre cubes in one layer.
This is 15cm³.
There are 2 layers of 15 centimetre cubes.
This is 30cm³. The volume of the cuboid is 30cm³.

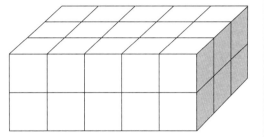

To find the volume of a cuboid, use the formula: $V = L \times W \times H$.

## Practise

(1) Find the volume of these cuboids. Use centimetres cubed (cm³) as units for the answer.

**a.**

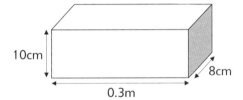

10cm    8cm    0.3m

_____

**b.**

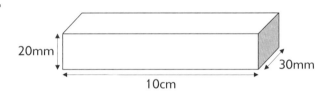

20mm    30mm    10cm

_____

**c.**

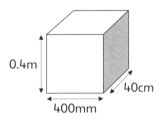

0.4m    40cm    400mm

_____

**d.**

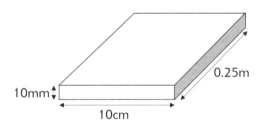

10mm    0.25m    10cm

_____

(2) Complete the table to find the measurements for these cuboids.

|     | Length | Width | Height | Volume |
|-----|--------|-------|--------|--------|
| a.  | 15cm   | 5cm   | 5cm    |        |
| b.  |        | 30cm  | 20cm   | 30 000cm³ |
| c.  | 50cm   |       | 5cm    | 3000cm³ |

**3** Two nets of cuboids are drawn on the square grid. Each square on the grid represents one square centimetre. Write the volumes of the cuboids.

**a.**
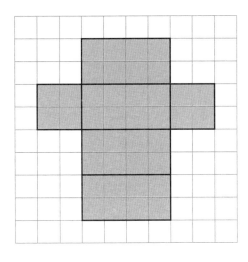

**b.**
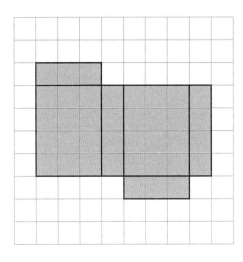

_____

_____

**4** A cuboid has length of 10cm, a width of 6cm and a height of 4cm. Its volume is 240cm³. Write the measurements of **two** other cuboids that have the same volume.

**a.** _____ × _____ × _____    **b.** _____ × _____ × _____

**5** An 8cm cube has the same volume as a cuboid with a length of 16cm and a width of 4cm. What is the height of the cuboid?   _____

 **Apply**

**6** Solve these problems.

**a.** Ava makes a cuboid with centimetre cubes. It is 18cm long, 4cm wide and 3cm high. Ava rearranges the centimetre cubes to make one large cube. How long is one side of the cube?   _____

**b.** Zola has a fish tank that is 70cm long, 40cm wide and 40cm tall. She fills the tank to 5cm below the top. How many litres of water does Zola add to the tank?   _____

**c.** Toby has some building blocks. Each block is 10cm long, 5cm wide and 5cm high. He uses 12 blocks to build a tower. What is the volume of the tower?   _____

**d.** Kai has a jug that holds $\frac{1}{2}$ a litre. He fills a cube-shaped tank that has 20cm sides. How many full jugs will it take to fill the tank?   _____

**Tip** If you need to convert between cm³ and litres, use the conversion 1000cm³ = 1 litre.

# Measurement word problems

## Practise

**1** Solve these problems.

**a.** A classroom is 4.5m long and 4m wide. What is the area of the classroom? _____

**b.** Louise needs to put a fence around a rectangular field. The field is 80m long and 65m wide. The field has two gates that are each 2.5m wide. What length of fencing does Louise need? _____

**c.** Oscar's toy box is the shape of a cuboid. It is 120cm long, 40cm wide and 50cm high. What is the volume of the toy box? _____

**d.** Mira arrives at the train station at ten to three in the afternoon. Her train is due to leave at 15:17. How long does she have to wait for the train to leave? _____

**e.** Amy and Harper share £48 so that Amy has half the amount Harper has. How much does Harper get? _____

**f.** Ted uses 2.4kg of flour to make 5 similar cakes. How many grams of flour are used for each cake? _____

**g.** A 225ml carton of juice costs 85p. Holly buys 12 cartons.

    **i.** How many litres of juice does Holly buy? _____

    **ii.** How much does Holly spend? _____

**h.** Jasmine runs the same route each day for a week. The route is 6750 metres long. How many kilometres does Jasmine run in total? _____

**i.** Faye has a roll of ribbon that is 5m long. She uses 150cm of ribbon to tie a present. How much ribbon does she have left? _____

**Extend**

**2** Solve these problems.

**a.** Mei buys a jumper and two similar T-shirts for £43.50.
The jumper costs £24. How much does each T-shirt cost? _____

**b.** Joe is going to the cinema. The film he is going to see starts
at 18:35 and lasts 208 minutes. When does the film end? _____

**c.** In a classroom, a set of drawers is 1200mm wide. The classroom is 7m wide.

  **i.** How many sets of drawers could fit along that wall? _____

  **ii.** How much space will be left when as many sets of drawers
  as possible are set along the wall? _____

**d.** Lottie has this block in a set of 3D shapes. It is a prism with a
shaded end face in the shape of a cross. The cross is made of
five squares with sides 3cm as shown by the dashed lines.

  **i.** What is the area of the end face? _____

  **ii.** What is the volume of the prism? _____

5cm

3cm

> **Tip** To find the volume of a prism, multiply the area of the end face by the depth.

**Apply**

**3** Solve these problems.

**a.** A pack of 4 cans of cola costs £2.25 and a pack of 6 cans of
cola costs £2.95. What is the difference between buying 12
cans of cola in packs of 4 or in packs of 6? _____

**b.** Chaya feeds her gerbil 20g of food a day. She buys a 1.25kg
bag of gerbil food. How many days will the bag of food last? _____

**c.** Sarim's rectangular lawn measures 22m by 15m. Sarim buys a bottle of lawn feed.
Its instructions say that to cover 5m$^2$ of lawn, he should add 10ml of lawn feed to
5 litres of water.

  **i.** How much lawn feed will Sarim need for his lawn? _____

  **ii.** How much water will he use? _____

**d.** Toni has cubic blocks with 3cm sides. She builds a larger
cube that has a volume of 1728cm$^3$. How many cubic blocks
does Toni use to build the larger cube? _____

# 2D shapes

## Remember

2D shapes have two dimensions: a length and a width. Sometimes different words are used for these, such as base and height. 2D shapes with straight sides are given special names according to the number of sides they have. For example: triangle (3), quadrilateral (4), pentagon (5), hexagon (6), heptagon (7) and octagon (8).

They may also be given special names according to the properties that they have. For example: quadrilaterals can be rectangles, squares, parallelograms, rhombuses, kites or trapeziums and all have four sides. A circle is also a 2D shape.

##  Practise

**1** Here are some quadrilaterals.

| rectangle | square | parallelogram | rhombus | isosceles trapezium | trapezium | kite |

**a.** A parallelogram is a quadrilateral with two pairs of parallel sides. Write the names of the shapes in the diagram that are also parallelograms.

_____

**b.** A kite has adjacent sides (sides next to each other) that are equal. Write the names of the shapes in the diagram that are also kites.

_____

**c.** The diagonals of a square are perpendicular. Write the names of any other shapes in the diagram that have perpendicular diagonals.

_____

**2** Calculate the radius of a circle with a diameter of 19cm. _____

**3** Calculate the diameter of a circle with a radius of 17.5cm. _____

**Tip** The circumference (*c*) is the outside edge of a circle. The diameter (*d*) is a line from edge to edge through the centre of a circle. The radius (*r*) is a line from the centre to the edge of the circle.

**Extend**

**4** These shapes are partly covered.

Which quadrilaterals could they be? Select from the shapes drawn in **Question 1**.

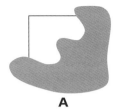 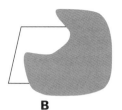

A          B

**a.** Quadrilateral A could be _____.

**b.** Quadrilateral B could be _____.

**5** Here are three shapes. Each shape has equal sides. Write how many lines of symmetry each shape has.

**a.** regular pentagon       **b.** regular octagon       **c.** dodecagon (12-sided shape)

_____             _____             _____

**6** Write the name of the only regular quadrilateral.        _____

 **Apply**

**7** Solve these problems.

**a.** Joey draws a square. He cuts identical isosceles triangles from each corner of the square. Write the names of **two** shapes that he could have made.

**i.** _____       **ii.** _____

**b.** Rose draws a rectangle that contains three circles that just touch each other and the sides of the rectangle. The radius of one circle is 4.5cm. What is the perimeter of the rectangle?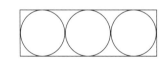

_____

**c.** Noah makes some statements about triangles. Explain why each statement is **not** correct.

**i.** All right-angled triangles are scalene triangles.

_____

**ii.** All isosceles triangles are acute-angled triangles.

_____

# Drawing 2D shapes

## Remember

When drawing 2D shapes, take care to draw accurately. This means using a ruler to draw the lengths correctly and a protractor or angle measurer to draw angles to the correct size. It is best to use a pencil so that mistakes can be erased. Think about the properties of 2D shapes when drawing.

 **Practise**

**1** These are square grids. Divide the grid into:

    **a.** two right-angled triangles and a parallelogram.

    **b.** two trapeziums and an isosceles triangle.

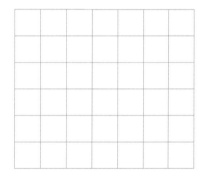 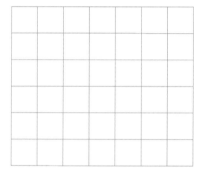

**2** Measure the lines to the nearest millimetre.

    **a.**

    **b.**

    **c.**

**3** Measure the angles to the nearest degree.

    **a.**

    **b.**

 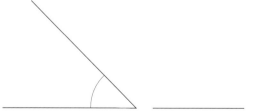

**Tip** Make sure that you line up your protractor or angle measurer carefully and that you begin counting from 0°.

# Extend

④ The line AB and the line CD cross at 35°. Draw another line EF that also crosses the line AB and is parallel to the line CD. Label the third line EF.

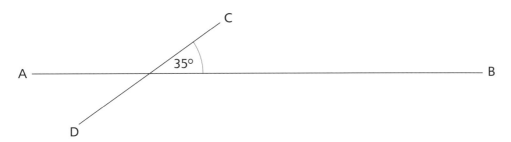

⑤ The base of a triangle has been drawn. One angle on the base is 40°. The other angle on the base is 35°. Complete the triangle by measuring the angles and drawing the two missing sides.

---

# Apply

⑥ Solve this problem.

**a.** Explain why Harpreet cannot draw these shapes.

    **i.** a triangle with sides of 15cm, 8cm and 7cm

_____

    **ii.** a triangle with two obtuse angles

_____

    **iii.** a parallelogram with angles of 35°, 45°, 135° and 145°

_____

⑦ Marcus says that it is impossible to draw a pentagon with a line of symmetry and three right angles. Show that Marcus is **not** correct by drawing on this grid.

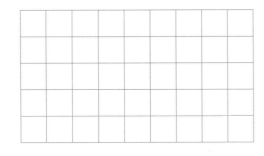

**Tip** Use the corners of the squares to draw the right angles, but remember that right angles do not always need to have horizontal and vertical sides.

# 3D shapes

## Remember

3D shapes have three dimensions. These are usually described as length, width and height. These are shapes that are solid and can be picked up and handled. 3D shapes may have flat faces or curved surfaces. Some of these shapes have special names.

Cuboids and cubes have six flat faces at right angles to each other.

Prisms have two identical end faces and these are joined by rectangular faces.

Pyramids have a base and triangular faces from each edge of the base that meet at an apex (vertex) above the base.

A face is a flat side of a 3D shape. An edge is where two faces meet. A vertex is where three or more edges meet.

## Practise

1. Here are some 3D shapes. For each shape give the number of faces, edges and vertices.

    **a.** hexagonal prism

    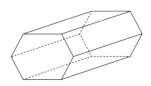

    _____ faces

    _____ edges

    _____ vertices

    **b.** cuboid

    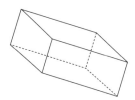

    _____ faces

    _____ edges

    _____ vertices

    **c.** pentagonal pyramid

    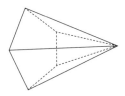

    _____ faces

    _____ edges

    _____ vertices

    **d.** pentagonal prism

    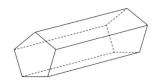

    _____ faces

    _____ edges

    _____ vertices

2. Write the names of the shape from the description.

    **a.** two circular end faces joined by one curved surface _____

    **b.** four triangular faces _____

    **c.** six square faces at right angles to each other _____

    **d.** one square face and four triangular faces _____

**Tip** Think of 3D shapes you know and see if the correct 2D shapes are listed.

**3** Asma makes some models of 3D shapes using straws and balls of plasticine. She has used 4 straws and 3 balls of plasticine for each shape. How many more straws and how many more balls of plasticine will she need to complete each shape?

**a.** This is going to be an octagonal prism.

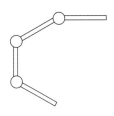

_____ more straws

_____ more balls of plasticine

**b.** This is going to be an octagonal pyramid.

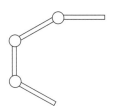

_____ more straws

_____ more balls of plasticine

**4** Tick to show whether each statement is true or false.

|  |  | True | False |
|---|---|---|---|
| **a.** | Some prisms do not have any rectangular faces. |  |  |
| **b.** | All pyramids must have at least three triangular faces. |  |  |
| **c.** | A cube is a special type of cuboid. |  |  |

 **Apply**

**5** Solve these problems.

**a.** **i.** Lily has two cubes of the same size. She joins them together so two faces always match exactly. She says that every time she joins them together, she will always make a cuboid. Is Lily correct? Explain your answer.

_____

**ii.** Lily gets an extra cube, so she now has three cubes. She joins them together. She says that every time she joins them together, she will always make a cuboid. Is Lily correct? Explain your answer.

_____

**b.** Two square-based pyramids fit on the square ends of a cuboid. How many faces, edges and vertices does the shape have?

_____ faces, _____ edges and _____ vertices

# Nets of 3D shapes

## Remember

A net shows all the faces of a 3D shape as though they had been unfolded and shown as a 2D shape.

This is a cube.     This is a net of a cube.

## Practise

**1** These shapes all have six squares. Circle the shapes that are nets of a cube.

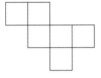    

**Tip** Imagine folding nets up to make the shapes. You could even draw them on paper, cut them out and fold them up.

  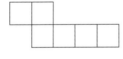  

  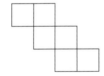  

**2** Draw lines to match the name of shape to its net.

  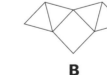  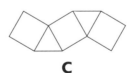  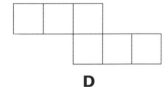

|  A |  B |  C |  D |

    cube       triangular prism     square-based pyramid    triangle-based pyramid

**3** Write the name of each shape.

    **a.** The shape that has a net of a pentagon and five triangles. _____

    **b.** The shape that has a net of two pentagons and five rectangles. _____

    **c.** The shape that has a net of two squares and four oblongs. _____

    **d.** The shape that has a net of two circles and one rectangle. _____

## Extend

**4** Draw the **one** missing face on these nets of cuboids.

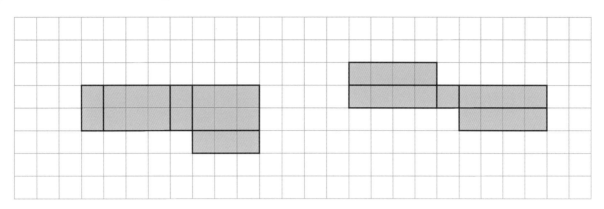

**5** This table shows the 2D shapes needed to make nets of 3D shapes. Complete the table. One has been done for you.

|   |   | Triangles | Rectangles | Pentagons | Hexagons |
|---|---|---|---|---|---|
| **a.** | triangular prism | 2 | 3 | 0 | 0 |
| **b.** | hexagonal pyramid |   |   |   |   |
| **c.** | pentagonal prism |   |   |   |   |
| **d.** | triangle-based pyramid |   |   |   |   |

## Apply

**6** Solve these problems.

**a.** A die is a cube. Yaz has this net for a die numbered 1 to 6. Three of the numbers are shown. The numbers on opposite sides of a die always add to 7. Write the missing numbers on the net.

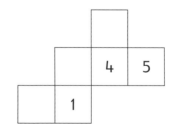

**b.** Yaz uses a different net for a cube. She marks one edge on each net in red. Circle the edge on each net that would join the marked edge on the cube.

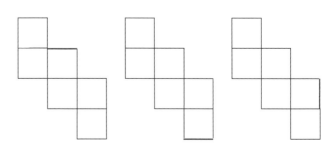

# Angles

## Remember

An angle is a measure of turn. Degrees (°) are used to measure angles. There are 360°
in a whole turn.

$\frac{1}{4}$ turn = 90°     This is a right angle.

$\frac{1}{2}$ turn = 180°     This is a straight angle or a straight line.

$\frac{3}{4}$ turn = 270°     This makes a whole turn with a right angle.

The angles of a triangle always add to 180°. The angles of a quadrilateral always add
to 360°.

## ✏ Practise

**(1)** Find these missing angles.

**a.**

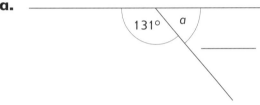

**b.**

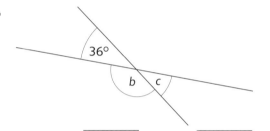

**c.**

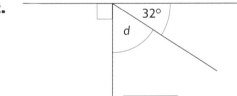

**d.**

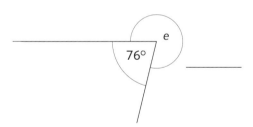

**e.**

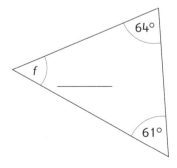

**f.**

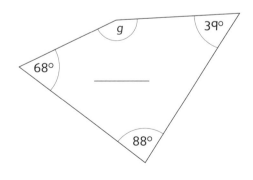

**Tip**   A small square in the corner of an angle is the symbol for a right angle.

# Extend

**(2)** Calculate the missing angles.

**a.** In a parallelogram, one of the angles is 47°.
Calculate the other three angles. _____ , _____ and _____

**b.** In an isosceles triangle, one of the angles is 56°. Calculate the other two angles.
Give **two** sets of answers.

    **i.** _____ and _____    **ii.** _____ and _____

**c.** In a quadrilateral, three of the angles are 95°, 63° and 38°.
What is the fourth angle? _____

**d.** In a trapezium, two angles are right angles and a third is 126°.
What is the fourth angle? _____

**(3)** In this triangle, one angle is x°. A second angle is twice as large (2x°) and the third angle is three times as large (3x°). What is the size of each angle?

**a.** x° = _____

**b.** 2x° = _____

**c.** 3x° = _____

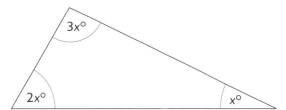

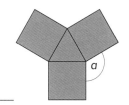

# Apply

**(4)** Solve these problems.

**a.** Andi is laying tiles. He begins with this pattern using an equilateral triangle and three congruent squares. What is the size of the missing angle a? _____

**b.** Sandhu has a piece of card in the shape of an isosceles triangle. He cuts it into two pieces. Calculate angles b, c and d.

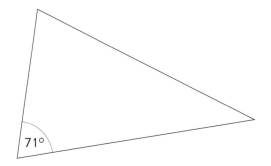

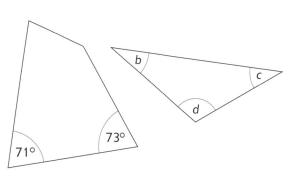

    **i.** b = _____    **ii.** c = _____    **iii.** d = _____

# Coordinate grids

Extend

## Remember

Coordinates show a specific point on a grid.

Each axis on a grid is usually numbered. An axis can show negative as well as positive numbers.

Coordinates are recorded using the number from the x-axis first. This is the horizontal axis. The number from the y-axis is shown second.

Coordinates are usually written in brackets with the numbers separated by a comma. The dot on this grid has the coordinates (−2, 1).

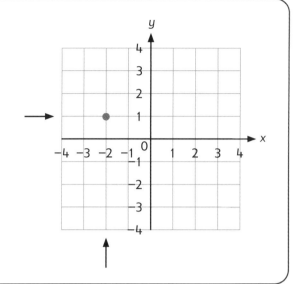

## Practise

**1** Write the coordinates of the points on this grid.

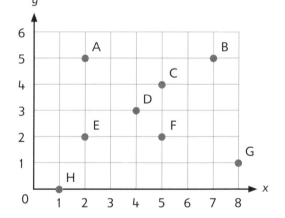

**a.** A = _____   **b.** B = _____

**c.** C = _____   **d.** D = _____

**e.** E = _____   **f.** F = _____

**g.** G = _____   **h.** H = _____

**Tip** Remember the coordinate from the x-axis is written before the coordinate from the y-axis.

**2** Plot and label these coordinates on the grid.

**a.** A at (6, 4)   **b.** B at (4, 6)

**c.** C at (1, 3)   **d.** D at (2, 4)

**e.** E at (4, 2)   **f.** F at (8, 4)

**g.** G at (6, 0)   **h.** H at (0, 3)

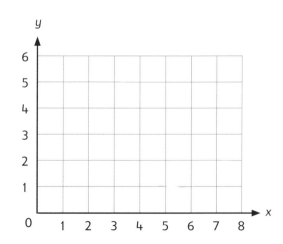

## ⟫ Extend

**3** Use this grid to answer **Questions 3a**, **b** and **c**.

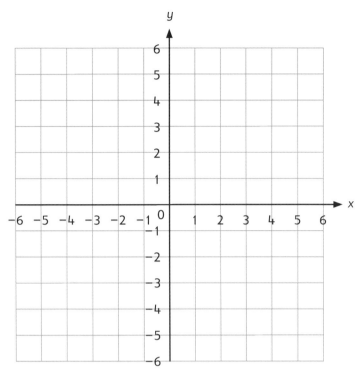

> **Tip** Connect the points as you plot them to make the sides of the shapes. Remember that the sides of squares and rectangles will always be perpendicular, so they will make right angles.

**a.** Plot three of the coordinates of a square: (2, 1), (4, 1) and (2, −1). Add the fourth vertex and draw the square.

**b.** Plot three of the coordinates of a rectangle: (−5, 2), (0, 2) and (−5, −2). Add the fourth vertex and draw the rectangle.

**c.** Plot the line from (−2, 1) to (1, 1). This is one side of a square. The square can be completed in different ways. What could the other two vertices of **one** possible square be?

_____ and _____

##  Apply

**4** Solve these problems.

**a.** Three vertices of a square are (10, 14), (14, 14) and (10, 10). What are the coordinates of the fourth vertex?  _____

**b.** Two equal, adjacent sides of a kite have vertices at (−8, 12), (−10, 8) and (−6, 8). What could the coordinates of the fourth vertex be?  _____

**c.** Three coordinates of a parallelogram are (−2, −3), (1, −3) and (0, −4). There are three possible coordinates for the fourth vertex. Give **two** possible vertices.

**i.** _____     **ii.** _____

# Reflection

## Remember

Shapes can be moved. One of the ways shapes can be moved is with a reflection. A reflection is a flip. The reflections are in a line of reflection or mirror line. All vertices must be the same distance from the mirror line after reflection as they were before.

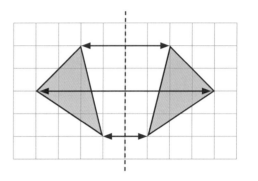

## Practise

**1** Tick the pairs of shapes that have been correctly reflected.

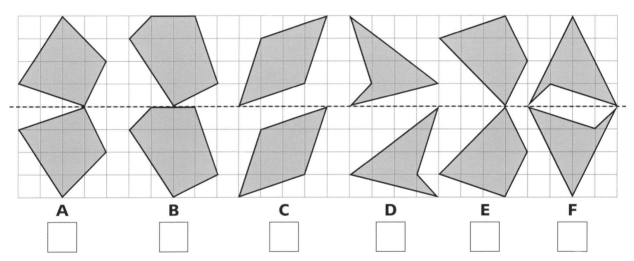

| A | B | C | D | E | F |
|---|---|---|---|---|---|
| ☐ | ☐ | ☐ | ☐ | ☐ | ☐ |

**2** Draw reflections of the shapes.

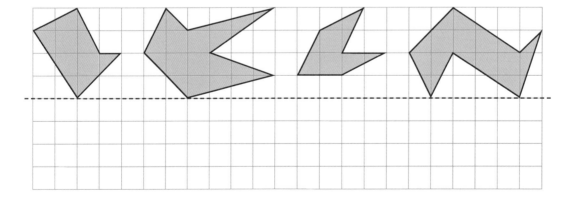

**3** Is this statement true or false? Circle **one**.

All reflected shapes must have an internal line of symmetry.       True          False

# Extend

**4** Draw the reflection of the shape.

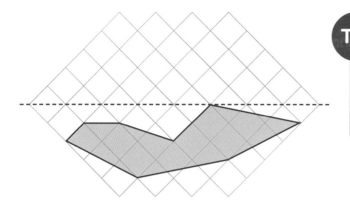

**Tip** Although the grid is at a different angle for this question, use the same method to reflect the shape. Reflect the points one at a time and join them as you go.

**5** These patterned shapes are reflected in the mirror lines. Complete the pattern.

**a.**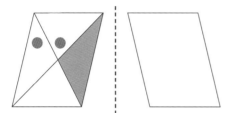

**b.**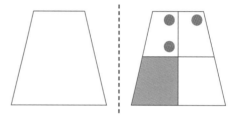

# Apply

**6** Draw the reflection of the shape.

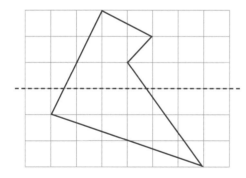

**Tip** This shape is on both sides of the mirror line to begin with, which means that its reflection will be on both sides of the mirror line too.

**7** The x- and y-axes are shown, along with shapes with the coordinates for their vertices. Each shape is reflected in the x-axis and then the y-axis. Write the coordinates for the final position of each shape.

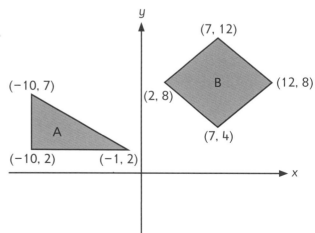

**a.** The new coordinates for A are

_____.

**b.** The new coordinates for B are

_____.

# Translation

Shapes can be moved. One of the ways shapes can be moved is with a translation. A translation is a slide in one or two directions. Translations are described by the number of units they move horizontally or vertically. This triangle has been translated 7 units (squares) right and 2 units down.

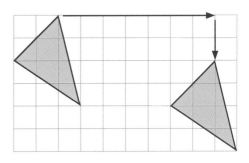

 **Practise**

(1) Tick the pairs of shapes that have been correctly translated.

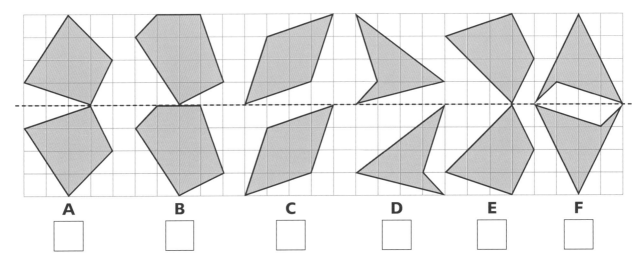

A      B      C      D      E      F

(2) Describe these translations by giving the number of units and the direction (left, right, up or down).

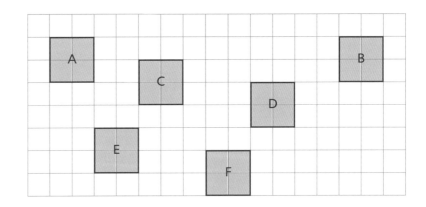

**a.** The translation of Square B to Square D _____

**b.** The translation of Square E to Square A _____

**c.** The translation of Square C to Square F _____

# Extend

**3** Draw the shapes in their new positions.

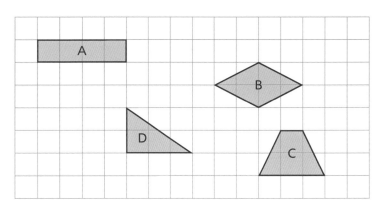

    **a.** Translate A 4 units right and 1 unit down.

    **b.** Translate B 8 units left and 4 units down.

    **c.** Translate C 1 unit left and 5 units up.

    **d.** Translate D 1 unit right and 1 unit down.

**4** A point on a coordinate grid has the coordinates (4, 7).

    **a.** The point is translated 6 units left and 10 units down. What are the new coordinates? _____

    **b.** The same point is translated 10 units left and 6 units down. What are the new coordinates? _____

# Apply

**5** Two triangles are shown with their coordinates. Describe the **two** possible translations.

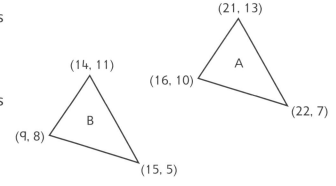

    **a.** A to B is a translation of _____ units left and _____ units down.

    **b.** B to A is a translation of _____ units right and _____ units up.

**6** Quadrilateral A has the coordinates (−8, 3), (7, 4), (−5, −3) and (6, −5).

    **a.** If Quadrilateral A is translated 6 units right and 5 units down, what are the coordinates of the quadrilateral in its new position?

    _____

    **b.** If Quadrilateral A is translated 3 units left and 7 units up, what are the coordinates of the quadrilateral in its new position?

    _____

# Constructing graphs

## Remember

Line graphs show continuous data, such as temperature. Line graphs are drawn using two axes that display the data. One of these axes, usually the x-axis, displays the time period for the data. Pie charts are graphs shown as circles. Sectors show the proportion of data in relation to the whole. For example: if 25 children out of 100 children are in Year 6, this would be shown as a quarter of the whole circle.

## Practise

(1) 48 children decide what they want to do on a school visit. Complete the pie chart with this data.

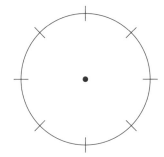

   **a.** 6 children want to visit a castle.

   **b.** 18 children want to visit a museum.

   **c.** 24 children want to visit the beach.

(2) Some builders build 120 houses. Complete the pie chart with this data using a protractor or angle measurer.

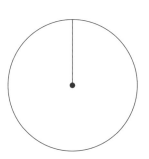

   **a.** 10 houses are bungalows.

   **b.** 20 houses are detached.

   **c.** 40 houses are semi-detached.

   **d.** 50 are terraced.

**Tip** There are 360° in a full turn. Use this information to divide the sectors for the pie chart.

(3) A line graph shows the monthly temperatures for a year. The lowest temperature was 2°C and the highest temperature was 32°C. Tick the best scale for the line graph. Tick **one**.

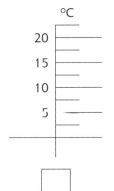 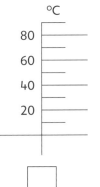 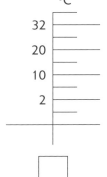 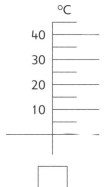 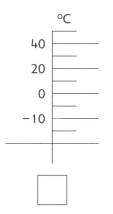

# Extend

④ This table shows the mean monthly temperatures in Delhi, India. Use this data to draw a line graph.

|  | January | February | March | April | May | June |
|---|---|---|---|---|---|---|
| Temp. (°C) | 14 | 16 | 22 | 28 | 30 | 34 |

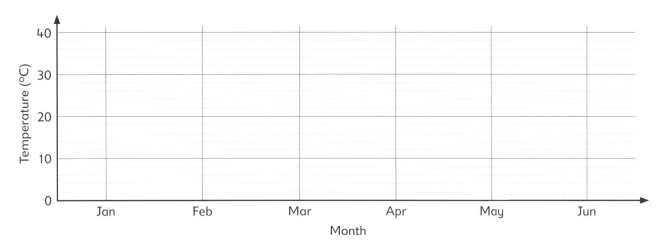

 **Apply**

⑤ Solve these problems.

a. Angus has surveyed children in his school and has found that 30 out of 100 children cycle to school each day. He is planning to draw a pie chart. He says that the sector to show the children who cycle will need to have an angle of 30° at the centre.
Is Angus correct? Give **one** reason for your answer.

_____

b. There are 62 children in Year 6 that take part in a survey. Issa says that $\frac{7}{10}$ of the children have a mobile phone. Issa is **not** correct. Explain why.

_____

c. Tara is drawing a line graph to show the temperature outside her classroom. She records the temperature every 2 hours. Here is part of the line graph.

Tara says that it must be 7°C at 09:00. Is Tara correct? Give **one** reason for your answer.

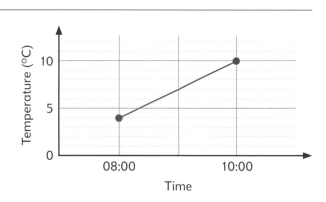

_____

# Pie charts

## Remember

Pie charts are graphs shown as circles. Sectors show the proportion of data in relation to the whole. For example: if 25 children out of 100 children are in Year 6, this would be shown as a quarter of the whole circle. Pie charts should indicate the total number that is represented by the whole pie chart. Some pie charts may use fractions of the whole. Others may use degrees to create the sectors for the pie chart. Sometimes interpreting the sector as a fraction is important; quarters, halves and three-quarters can be identified quickly.

## Practise

**1** This pie chart shows the types of lunch 120 children eat at school. Write how many children ate these meals.

   **a.** sandwiches _____

   **b.** salad _____

   **c.** a vegetarian meal _____

   **d.** a hot meal _____

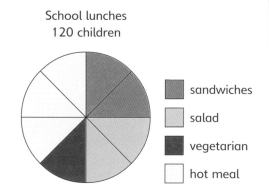

School lunches
120 children

sandwiches
salad
vegetarian
hot meal

**2** This pie chart shows how 120 children would like to celebrate the end of Year 6. Write how many children picked these options.

   **a.** visit a theme park _____

   **b.** visit the cinema _____

   **c.** have a prom _____

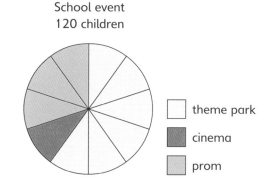

School event
120 children

theme park
cinema
prom

**3** Year 6 counted the birds visiting a bird table outside their classroom.

   **a.** How many sparrows were seen? _____

   **b.** Twice as many blackbirds as starlings were seen. How many blackbirds were seen? _____

   **c.** Estimate the number of magpies seen. _____

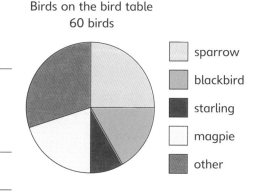

Birds on the bird table
60 birds

sparrow
blackbird
starling
magpie
other

# Extend

**4** This pie chart shows the instruments in a brass band.

    **a.** How many trombones are there?   _____

    **b.** The angle for the sector showing tubas is 72°.

       How many tubas are there?   _____

    **c.** The sector for horns is 20% of the pie chart.

       How many horns are there?   _____

    **d.** There are six times as many cornets as drums.

       **i.** How many cornets are there?   _____

       **ii.** How many drums are there?   _____

Brass band instruments
200 instruments

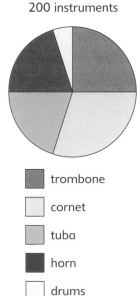

- trombone
- cornet
- tuba
- horn
- drums

**Tip** Degrees can be turned into a fraction. Put the number of degrees in a sector over the number of degrees in a circle. Simplify this fraction as usual.

# Apply

**5** These pie charts shows the results of two school football teams over one season.

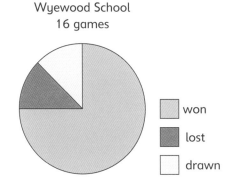

Howgreen School
24 games

- won
- lost
- drawn
- abandoned

Wyewood School
16 games

- won
- lost
- drawn

    **a.** Which team won the most games and by how many games?

    _____

    **b.**  **i.** How many games did Howgreen School draw?   _____

       **ii.** How many games did Wyewood School draw?   _____

    **c.** In the games they lost, Wyewood School scored a mean of 3 goals. How many goals did they score in total in the games they lost?   _____

# Line graphs

## Remember

Line graphs show continuous data, such as temperature. Line graphs are drawn using two axes that display the data. One of these axes, usually the x-axis, displays the time period for the data. Some line graphs may display more than one line or more than one set of data. Read a line graph by following the horizontal or vertical lines from the axes and finding the values of that point.

 **Practise**

1. This line graph shows the temperature in a ski resort. The temperature is recorded every two hours.

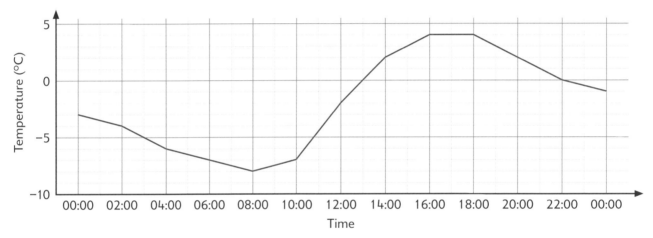

   **a.** Find the temperatures at these times.

   **i.** 16:00 _____    **ii.** 22:00 _____

   **iii.** 02:00 _____    **iv.** 08:00 _____

   **b.** At what time did the temperature that was recorded reach these values?

   **i.** the lowest value _____

   **ii.** the highest value _____

   **c.** For approximately how many hours that day was the temperature:

   **i.** above 0°C? _____    **ii.** below −5°C? _____

   **d.** Tom says that the temperature rose to 0°C at exactly 13:00. Explain why Tom might **not** be correct.

   _____

# Extend

2. The line graph shows Dev's heart rate (the dashed line), with the scale on the left vertical axis. The graph also shows the distance Dev has cycled (the solid line), with the scale on the right vertical axis.

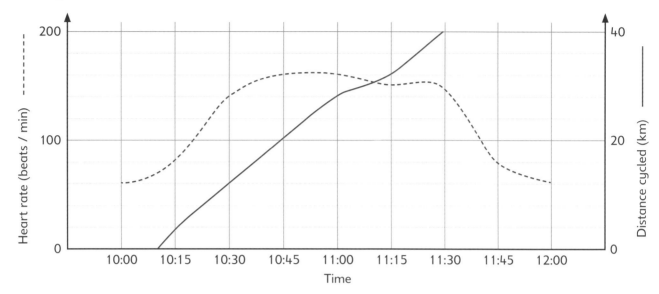

a. Estimate Dev's heart rate at 10:00. _____

b. Estimate the time that Dev set off on his cycle ride. _____

c. Estimate Dev's highest heart rate. _____

d. Estimate the time Dev took to complete his cycle ride. _____

e. At what time had Dev completed half of the distance? _____

# Apply

3. Answer these questions using the graph in **Question 2**.

a. In which quarter of an hour period did Dev cycle the
shortest distance? _____ to _____

b. Estimate the distance Dev cycled between 10:30 and 11:15. _____

c. Estimate the fall in Dev's heart rate from 11:00 to 11:30. _____

d. Estimate Dev's heart rate after he had cycled 10km. _____

e. Estimate how far Dev had cycled when his heart rate
reached 100 beats / min. _____

f. After Dev finished his cycle ride, estimate how long it took
for his heart rate to return to the rate at 10:00. _____

# Mean

## Practise

1. These bar models show how to calculate the mean of a set of numbers. Complete the bar models with the missing numbers.

   a.

   | 22 | | 20 |
   |----|----|----|
   | 57 | | |
   | | | |

   b.

   | 15 | 18 | 13 | |
   |------|------|------|------|
   | | | | |
   | 18.5 | 18.5 | 18.5 | 18.5 |

2. Find the means of these sets of numbers.

   a.  7        14       24        2        8        _____

   b.  15       120      55        74                _____

   c.  324      625      185                         _____

   d.  2.4      0.8      4.1       2.7      3.5       _____

3. Solve these problems.

   a. The mean of three numbers is 15. Two of the numbers are 7 and 21. What is the third number?        _____

   b. The mean of four numbers is 12. Three of the numbers total 20. What is the fourth number?        _____

**Tip**  Work out the total by multiplying the mean by the number of numbers.

# Extend

**4** The mean of three whole numbers is 4 and one of the numbers is 8. What could the other two numbers be? Give **two** possible combinations.

   **a.** _____ and _____          **b.** _____ and _____

**5** The mean of four whole numbers is 3 and three of the numbers are the same. What could the four numbers be? Give **two** possible combinations.

   **a.** _____, _____, _____ and _____

   **b.** _____, _____, _____ and _____

**6** Here are a set of number cards.

| 1 | 2 | 3 | 4 | 5 | 6 | 7 | 8 |

   **a.** The mean of three of the numbers is 6. What could the numbers be?

   _____, _____ and _____

   **b.** The mean of four of the numbers is 6. What could the numbers be?

   _____, _____, _____ and _____

# Apply

**7** Solve these problems.

   **a.** Four classes have a mean size of 30 children. Three of the classes have the same number of children and they have over 30 but under 35 children. How many children could be in the fourth class? _____

   **b.** Katie has taken four spelling tests. Her mean score is 75%. What score must Katie achieve in the fifth test so her mean score is 80%? _____

   **c.** The mean height of a group of 7 children is 148cm. A child whose height is 142cm leaves the group. What is the mean height of the six remaining children? _____

   **d.** A train comprises nine coaches. The mean number of passengers in a coach is 67 passengers. Three coaches have 64 passengers each and four coaches have 70 passengers each. How many passengers could be in the remaining two coaches?

   _____ and _____

# Final practice

The Final practice assesses knowledge from every unit of this book. Work through the questions carefully and try to answer each one. The target time for completing these questions is 1 hour. The answers can be downloaded from the **Schofield & Sims** website.

**(1)** These are nets of 3D shapes. Write the names of the shapes.

a.

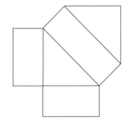

b.

_____   _____   2 marks

**(2)** Calculate:

a. $\frac{3}{8} + \frac{2}{3} =$ _____

b. $\frac{9}{10} - \frac{1}{4} =$ _____

c. $2\frac{4}{5} - \frac{2}{3} =$ _____

d. $3\frac{11}{12} + 1\frac{5}{8} =$ _____   4 marks

**(3)** Calculate:

a. 30% of 250 = _____

b. $\frac{4}{5}$ of 600 = _____

c. $\frac{7}{8}$ of 400 = _____

d. 75% of 2400 = _____   4 marks

**(4)** Circle the numbers where the digit 4 has a value of forty thousand.

34 952        1 542 937        482 019        2 496 703        48 013        647 031        2 marks

**(5)** The temperature in a freezer is 15°C less than the temperature in the fridge, which is 15°C less than the temperature in the kitchen. The temperature in the kitchen is 21°C. What is the temperature in the freezer?

_____   2 marks

**(6)** Find the unknown values in these equations.

a. $23 + a = 41$        $a =$ _____

b. $b - 14 = 27$        $b =$ _____

c. $4c = 84$        $c =$ _____

d. $\frac{d}{6} = 12$        $d =$ _____   4 marks

# Final practice

**(7)** Alan has a rectangular lawn that is 30 metres long and 22 metres wide. He is planning to lay a diagonal path across the lawn dividing it into two identical triangles. The area of the path is shaded in the diagram.
What is the area of the path? _____

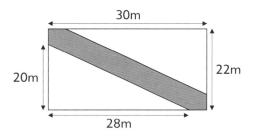

3 marks

**(8)** If 5 miles ≈ 8 kilometres, approximately how many miles are in 96km?

_____ 1 mark

**(9)** Calculate:

**a.** 1728 × 37 = _____          **b.** 6880 ÷ 32 = _____          2 marks

**(10)** Melissa has 125 counters and 20 of the counters are red.

**a.** Write the number of red counters as a fraction of all the counters. Write the fraction in its simplest terms.     _____

**b.** Write the red counters as a percentage of all the counters.     _____ 2 marks

**(11)** Write these fractions, decimals and percentages in order from smallest to largest.

35%          $\frac{3}{5}$          0.53          $\frac{5}{4}$          0.3

_____ 1 mark

**(12)** Calculate:

**a.** 50 + 200 ÷ 50 = _____          **b.** 100 − 40 × 2 = _____

**c.** (50 + 200) ÷ 50 = _____          **d.** (20 + 20) × (2 + 2) = _____ 4 marks

**(13)** Zara has completed five arithmetic practice tests.

Her scores in the practices are:     70%     78%     73%     92%     82%

**a.** Find the mean percentage.     _____

**b.** Zara completes a sixth practice test. She wants to increase her mean score to 80%. What score will she need to achieve to reach a mean of 80%?     _____ 2 marks

# Final practice

**(14)** This pie chart shows the texts that Manisha sends to her friends. She sends most texts to three friends, Abena, Tanya and Jill, and she sends more texts to other friends. Manisha sends six times as many texts to other friends as she does to Jill.

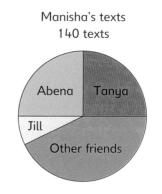

Manisha's texts
140 texts

How many texts did Manisha send to these people?

**a.** Tanya _____

**b.** Jill _____

**c.** Other friends _____

3 marks

**(15)** Reflect this shape in the *y*-axis and then in the *x*-axis. Draw the shape in its final position and label the final image A.

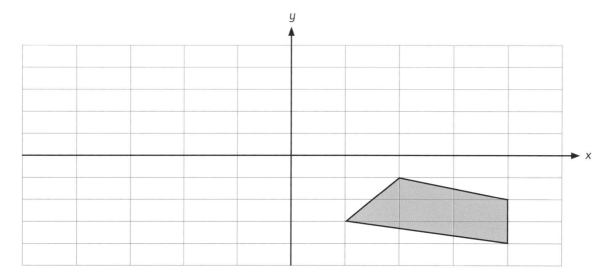

1 mark

**(16)** Find the missing angles.

**a.** A shaded equilateral triangle is surrounded by three isosceles triangles.

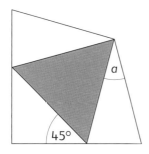

45°

$a =$ _____

**b.** Two identical parallelograms share a common side.

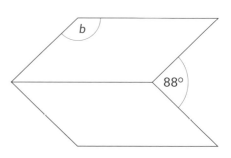

*b*

88°

$b =$ _____

2 marks

**17** Ms Mandal is ordering some new books for her classroom. She has £400 to spend. She buys 20 books that cost £6.99 each and 20 books that cost £8.99 each. She also wants to buy some books that cost £4.99 each. How many books that cost £4.99 each can Ms Mandel buy? _____ 3 marks

**18** Calculate:

**a.** $\frac{2}{3} \times \frac{3}{5} =$ _____

**b.** $\frac{4}{5} \div 4 =$ _____ 2 marks

**19** Give these amounts as decimals.

**a.** $\frac{4}{5} =$ _____

**b.** $45\% =$ _____ 2 marks

**20** Mandeep buys 10 boxes each with 100 pens for £50.
What is the cost of each pen? _____ 1 mark

**21** **a.** Leo uses 24 one-centimetre square tiles to make a rectangle. Circle the possible perimeters of the rectangles that Leo could make.

20cm          30cm          40cm          50cm          60cm

**b.** Next, Leo uses one-centimetre square tiles to make rectangles with a perimeter of 24cm. Circle the possible areas of the rectangles that Leo could make.

28cm²          30cm²          32cm²          34cm²          36cm²          2 marks

**22** Here are the names of some 3D shapes. Circle the names of the shapes that have six faces. Circle **two**.

triangular prism          cuboid          pentagonal prism          triangle-based pyramid          pentagonal pyramid          2 marks

**23** Rory and three friends have a meal. The food costs £72.80, the drinks cost £14.20 and they decide to leave a £10 tip. They share the cost equally. How much do they each pay? _____ 1 mark

# Final practice

(24) Lola draws this net of a cuboid on squared paper. Each square represents one square centimetre.

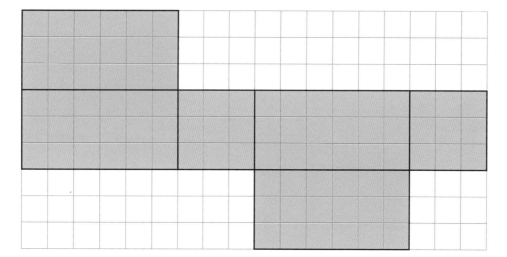

Write the volume of the cuboid. _____ 1 mark

(25) Jian is using a map with a scale of 1:50 000. On the map, the distance of a walk is 3.5cm. How far is the walk in real life? _____ 1 mark

(26) The instructions for the cooking time of a chicken in minutes are given by the formula 40k + 30, where k is the mass of the chicken in kilograms.

   **a.** Calculate the cooking time for a 3.5kg chicken in hours and minutes. _____

   **b.** Calculate the mass of a chicken if its cooking time is 2 hours and 20 minutes. _____ 2 marks

(27) These letters are different positive whole numbers. What could the values of the letters be? Give **three** solutions for each.

   **a.** 3a + 2b = 30

      a = _____ b = _____

      a = _____ b = _____

      a = _____ b = _____

   **b.** 2c × d = 48

      c = _____ d = _____

      c = _____ d = _____

      c = _____ d = _____ 4 marks

**Total:**

60 marks